# The Antinomies of Antonio Gramsci

# THE ANTINOMIES OF
# ANTONIO GRAMSCI

Perry Anderson

**VERSO**
London • New York

First published in paperback by Verso 2020
© Perry Anderson 2017, 2020
Translation of Athos Lisa's report © Eleanor Chiari 2017, 2020

1 3 5 7 9 10 8 6 4 2

**Verso**
UK: 6 Meard Street, London W1F 0EG
US: 20 Jay Street, Suite 1010, Brooklyn, NY 11201
versobooks.com

Verso is the imprint of New Left Books

ISBN-13: 978-1-78663-373-6
ISBN-13: 978-1-78663-375-0 (US EBK)
ISBN-13: 978-1-78664-374-3 (UK EBK)

**British Library Cataloguing in Publication Data**
A catalogue record for this book is available from the British Library

**Library of Congress Cataloging-in-Publication Data**
A catalog record for this book is available from the Library of Congress
Library of Congress Control Number: 2020935990

Typeset in Minion Pro by MJ &N Gavan, Truro, Cornwall
Printed and bound by CPI Group (UK) Ltd, Croydon, CR0 4YY

# CONTENTS

# PREFACE

No Italian thinker enjoys a greater fame today than Antonio Gramsci. If academic citations and internet references are any guide, he is more influential than Machiavelli. The bibliography of articles and books about him now runs to some 20,000 items. Amid this avalanche, is any compass possible? The *Prison Notebooks* first became available, thematically pre-packaged and politically expurgated, in Italy in the later 1940s. The first extensive translation from them into any language came in the early 1970s, with *Selections* in English produced by Quintin Hoare and Geoffrey Nowell Smith, giving them a global readership in what is still probably the most widely consulted single version of his writings. Some four decades later, the history of their worldwide reception is itself a scholarly topic, covering a vast span of usages.[1] The scale of this appropriation, in an epoch so unlike that in which Gramsci lived and thought, has owed much to two features of his legacy that set it apart from that of any other revolutionary of his time.

The first was its multidimensionality. The range of topics covered in the *Prison Notebooks*—the history of leading

---

1   See, among much else, the collections *Gramsci in Europa e in America*, Bari 1995, and *Gramsci in Asia e in Africa*, Cagliari 2010.

European states; the structure of their ruling classes; the character of their dominion over the ruled; the function and variation
of intellectuals; the experience of workers and the outlook of
peasants; the relations between state and civil society; the latest
forms of production and consumption; questions of philosophy
and education; the interconnexions between traditional or
avant-garde and popular or folkloric culture; the construction of nations and the survival of religions; and, not least, the
ways and means of passing beyond capitalism and sustaining
socialism—had, and has, no equal in the theoretical literature
of the left. The range was not only topical but spatial, since Italy
combined an advanced capitalist industry in the North with an
archaic pre-capitalist society in the South, and the *Notebooks*
came from a direct experience of both, capable in another time
of speaking to First and Third World readers alike. There was a
lot to choose from.

The second magnetic attraction of this writing lay in its frag-
mentation. In prison, Gramsci's notes were laconic, exploratory
jottings for works he was never able to compose in freedom. That
made them, as David Forgacs would point out, suggestive rather
than conclusive, inviting imaginative reconstruction after his
death, into one kind of totalisation or another.[2] Less binding than
a finished theory, they were the more appealing to interpreters
of every sort—a score inviting improvisation. In that attraction
lay, inevitably, also a temptation. What were the limits beyond
which the score itself was broken? That was one basic question
the essay below set out to address. At this date, some explanation
of its origins, aims and reception is needed. As a study of central
political concepts in Gramsci, it followed the reception of his

---

2　'Gramsci and Marxism in Britain', *New Left Review* I/176, July–August
　1989, p. 71.

work in the *New Left Review* of the early sixties, historically the first sustained attempt to make use of it outside his homeland. Concerned with analysis of the past and present of British society, this body of writing set out to put Gramsci's ideas to work more than to expound them. But soon afterwards, the journal began to publish translations and presentations of the canon of a Western Marxism that had developed in Europe outside the Soviet Union after the October Revolution, still vital—Lukács, Sartre, Adorno, Althusser were all active—at the time, with the aim of explicating and assessing its major thinkers.[3] Gramsci occupied a central place in this line. A product of that collective project was an essay that I published in 1974 attempting to resume the tradition, *Considerations on Western Marxism*.

A year later the first critical edition of the notebooks Gramsci composed in prison appeared in Italy, the fruit of years of meticulous work by Valentino Gerratana, a Communist scholar of outstanding sobriety and dignity. With this in hand, in late 1976 I wrote the text that ensues. The intention of 'Antinomies' was twofold, philological and historical: to look closely at the usage of central concepts in the *Prison Notebooks*, in a way that had not been done before, and to reconstruct the political contexts in which they originated and to which their meanings referred. The effect of doing so was, equally, twofold: to show the oscillations and contradictions in even, or perhaps particularly, the most striking and original themes of the *Notebooks*, with the intelligible reasons for these; and to demonstrate that, politically speaking, Gramsci was a revolutionary of Leninist stamp, whose strategic thought could only be understood within the parameters of the Third International and its debates.

---

3   See the essays collected in *Western Marxism: A Critical Reader*, London 1978.

Conceived as a sequel to *Considerations*, 'Antinomies' was composed in late 1976, and came out in *New Left Review* at the beginning of 1977. The following year it was published as a book in Italy under the title *Ambiguità di Gramsci*. There the Italian Communist Party had for some time declared that the way forward for the party and the country lay in a Historic Compromise with Christian Democracy, and in the summer of 1976 had achieved its highest ever level of electoral support, with over a third of the vote. In the wake of this success it was now backing a government of 'National Solidarity' led by Giulio Andreotti. This was a turn that in different ways had its counterpart in most of the Communist parties of Western Europe. Theorised as Eurocommunism by the Spanish party leader Santiago Carrillo, then helping to restore the Bourbon monarchy in Madrid, it was reproduced in its fashion by the Communist party in France, where the new doctrine had early adepts. Common to all variants was rejection of the principles on which the Third International had been founded, and commitment henceforward to gradual parliamentary reforms as the West European path to socialism; the Italian version adding a declaration of loyalty to NATO. In these conditions, the image of Gramsci—for the PCI, a national icon who could not be casually abandoned—had to be adjusted to the needs of the time, as a far-sighted precursor of the party's conversion to peaceful, incremental progress towards more advanced forms of democracy.

The Italian Socialist Party, under its new leader Bettino Craxi, did not, however, intend to let itself be marginalised by the Historic Compromise, and soon showed its ability to wrong-foot its larger rival. An early sign was the appearance in the autumn of 1976 of four articles in its monthly journal *Mondoperaio* by leading intellectuals—two historians, Massimo

Salvadori and Ernesto Galli della Loggia, and two philosophers, Norberto Bobbio and Lucio Colletti—congratulating the PCI on its new outlook, but calling on it to abandon the pretence that this had anything to do with Gramsci, who had been a dedicated revolutionary committed to the overthrow of the very liberal democracy to which the PCI had now at last rallied, as it became—a development which was entirely positive—for all practical purposes a reformist party in the tradition of Kautsky and European social democracy.[4] Put on the defensive, the PCI—which had been organising its own discussion to explain how its current positions were a creative development of the heritage of Gramsci—at first responded testily, then mindful of the need for national solidarity, more temperately but for the most part lamely, in early 1977. These exchanges overlapped with the appearance of 'Antinomies' in *New Left Review*. But not following the Italian political scene closely enough at that point, I was unaware of them.

Later that year, to commemorate the fortieth anniversary of Gramsci's death, the PCI organised its largest-ever conference on his thought. Held in Florence, and attended by numerous foreign participants, it marked, in the words of the richest history of the

---

4   *Egemonia e democrazia. Gramsci e la questione comunista nel dibat-tito di Mondoperaio*, Rome 1977, pp. 33–91. Salvadori had just (1976) published what remains by far the best study of Kautsky, translated into English in 1979 as *Kautsky and the Socialist Revolution, 1880–1938*—a fundamental work; Bobbio's manifesto *Quale socialismo?* also appeared in 1976—translated into English a decade later as *Which Socialism?*; Galli della Loggia would go on to produce the most striking work on Italian national identity, *L'identità italiana* (1996); Colletti, a member of the PCI from 1954 to 1964, had caused a considerable stir with the publication in book form of an interview conducted with him by *New Left Review* in 1974 (I/86, July–August 1974), which came out in Italy a year later as *Intervista politico-filosofica*, and was attacked in one of the PCI broadsides on the *Mondoperaio* symposium as a tap-root of its mischief.

reception of Gramsci in Italy, the apogee of his influence in the public life of the country. But, as the same account added, also the moment of its crisis.[5] For this was also the year of the widespread student and youth revolt against the Historic Compromise and all that it stood for, which became the 'Autonomia'. In February, the head of the PCI's trade union wing, who had told workers they must make economic sacrifices to prop up the National Solidarity government, was driven off the campus of Rome University amid angry scenes, and by the autumn Bologna was the stage of a virtual uprising. The Autonomia would fade, but the PCI never recovered from the alienation its connubium with Christian Democracy caused in the most politicised spirits of the younger generation. By the end of 1978 the failure of the Historic Compromise even on its own terms—the DC had taken Communist votes and yielded nothing in return—was obvious, and the PCI was duly punished at the elections the following year, beginning its slow descent towards dissolution.

The publication of *Ambiguità di Gramsci* in the spring of 1978 thus came at a juncture of continuing insistence by the PCI that its support for National Solidarity was thoroughly Gramscian, and a revolt against both the political line and the whole culture of the PCI by radical forces of a new generation to the left of it. For the latter, Gramsci was an irrelevance. For the former, any reminder of his connexion with Bolshevism could only be an embarrassment to the pursuit of a marriage with Christian Democracy. Logically, the book was ignored by the one and dismissed by the other.[6]

---

5    See Guido Liguori, *Gramsci Conteso. Interpretazioni, dibattiti e polemiche 1922–2012*, Rome 2012, pp. 269–72. This creditably balanced account is the work of a devoted member of the party, loyal to the memory of the PCI as it once was.

6    Amid the cross-currents of the time, individual figures often changed

Some six years later, however—by this time the Historic Compromise had been abandoned, though it was never repudiated—a reply was forthcoming. *L'officina gramsciana* marked the debut of a party intellectual with a future, Gianni Francioni. Proposing a reconstruction of the *Prison Notebooks* based on an attempt to determine as far as possible the precise chronological sequence of their composition, its aim was twofold: to dismantle the order of the critical edition produced by Gerratana, and to refute 'Antinomies', an exercise to which the latter part of the book was dedicated.[7] So far as the first went, the battery of tables and charts designed to establish the novelty and importance of Francioni's findings left Gerratana politely unpersuaded.[8] Lacking any reference to the trajectory of the actual conditions, physical and moral, in which Gramsci had to write in prison, the result says much less about the history of his composition than the acute and moving account of it by another scholar, Raul Mordenti, in the following decade.[9]

As to Francioni's other aim, the guiding principles behind his argument were affirmation of the essential coherence of

positions. Colletti, in the decade from 1964 to 1974 an eloquent critic of the PCI from the left, had by 1977 moved close to the PSI on its right. On reading 'Antinomies', he wrote to me saying he thought well of it and was recommending its publication in Italy with the house that had produced his interview, but that he himself had decided that it was necessary to rethink everything *ab imis*: letter, 1/6/1977. Much later, he would be elected to parliament on the centre-right list led by Silvio Berlusconi.

7 *L'officina gramsciana. Ipotesi sulla struttura dei 'Quaderni del carcere'*, Naples 1984: pp. 17–146 devoted to the first task, pp. 149–228 to the second.

8 *Gramsci. Problemi di metodo*, Rome 1997, 'Impaginazione e analisi dei "Quaderni"', pp. 143–53.

9 'Quaderni del carcere di Antonio Gramsci', in Alberto Asor Rosa (ed.), *Letteratura italiana*, Vol IV, Turin 1996, pp. 553–629. It is enough to compare Mordenti's analytic table and biographical comments, pp. 580–2 ff., with Francioni's appendix at pp. 137–46 to see the difference.

Gramsci's conceptual apparatus, and abstraction of it from any significant historical context; the first revolving around reiteration of the claim earlier advanced by a French stalwart of Eurocommunism, Christine Buci-Glucksmann, that contradictions in Gramsci's handling of the terms 'state' and 'civil society' disappeared once it was realised that he arrived at the notion of an 'enlarged' or 'integral' state encompassing both. The second involved a taboo on all evidence, however plain, that Gramsci's political outlook had by then virtually nothing in common with what the PCI had become. Chronological quibbles added little to the case.[10] As an enterprise in local apologetics, *L'officina gramsciana* was soon overtaken by events, as the party lurched towards its end. Three years later, on the fiftieth anniversary of Gramsci's death in 1987, Colletti could remark with relief that the left in Italy was now universally reformist, but Gramsci had never been, and the party had therefore rightly taken an all but irreversible distance from him. Within the PCI, no less an authority than Aldo Schiavone, director of the Gramsci Institute itself, concurred: in the overall politics of the party, he declared, not a single Gramscian idea was left.[11] Nor, it might be said, any other idea of moment in those who led it to extinction soon afterwards.

In Italy, the disappearance of the PCI has not meant loss of public interest in its greatest thinker. Too many careers,

---

10  Francioni's *pièce de résistance* was the objection that my treatment of three different usages of 'hegemony' in the *Notebooks* did not respect the order in which they first appeared in them. In fact, since I remarked that they were simultaneously at work in Gramsci's writing across the span of the notebooks, an analytic rather than a diachronic account of them was logical.

11  'Oggi non troviamo più una sola delle indicazioni politiche gramsciane alla base della politica complessiva del Pci'. See Liguori, *Gramsci conteso*, p. 310.

institutional or academic, remained invested in his person and work for the Gramsci industry in the country to close down along with the party that had given rise to it. Across the nineties and into the new century an indefatigable flow of exegesis has continued, in a philology now detached from current—if not always past—politics, culminating in the inception of an Edizione Nazionale of Gramsci's *opera omnia*, 'under the High Patronage of the President of the Republic', in 2007. Planned to total some nineteen volumes, a decade later just three have so far appeared, two of them simply translations from other writers by Gramsci, a rate at which the project could expect completion around 2070. Responsibility for volumes to contain in due course the *Prison Notebooks* has been entrusted to Francioni, fulfilling his ambition of supplanting the work of Gerratana, a scholar of an older style of integrity cold-shouldered by the legatees of his party.[12] Misgivings about the enterprise have been expressed by scholars attached to the memory of Gramsci in less marmoreal mode. Francioni's proposed rearrangements of the *Notebooks* have come under fire as arbitrary personal decisions, serving in one case—already on display—a concealed political intent with no philological foundation; while the monumental character of a National Edition, product of a decree of the Ministry of Culture,

---

12 In an incident worthy of Balzac, out of whose pages his successors could step, he was not even invited to the sixtieth anniversary commemoration of Gramsci's death. Born in Sicily in 1919, Gerratana joined the Resistance in Rome at the age of twenty-four, fighting in GAP (Gruppi di Azione Patriottica) and helping to organise the reconstruction of the PCI in the city. He was a friend and contemporary of Giaime Pintor, one of the most gifted writers of his generation, killed in 1943, whose posthumous collection *Il sangue d'Europa* Gerratana edited and introduced in 1950. Anglophone readers can get a sense of Gerratana's qualities as an intellectual historian from essays on Rousseau and Voltaire, Marx and Darwin, Lenin and Stalin, Althusser and Heidegger, translated in *New Left Review*, I/86, I/101–3, I/106, I/111. He died in 2000.

has prompted fears even among otherwise sympathetic critics that its effect risks official mummification of Gramsci.[13]

The most conspicuous other body of literature on Gramsci in Italy has been of an entirely different tenor, this one concerned—in recent times, to virtual paroxysm—with biographical questions about his personal life and political fate. These have surfaced as what was once tight party control of archives held in Rome has loosened, if still selectively, and what were formerly closed dossiers in Moscow have opened, if incompletely. New documentary evidence has come to light about the Russian family into which he married, the roles of Piero Sraffa and his sister-in-law Tatiana Schucht in his communications with the party while in prison, the actions taken towards him by the PCI and the Comintern in those years, the fate of his notebooks after his death, and much else. The copious literature all this has produced contains much of interest. But it has been persistently vitiated by two opposite instrumental motives.[14] Communism may have disappeared in Italy, but anti-communism has not: much of this biographical production serves simply as a stick with which to beat the PCI or Togliatti, not matter how long the

---

13  Liguori, *Gramsci conteso*, pp. 337–43, 418–20: Francioni's proposed alterations of Notebook 10 deprecated as a montage to change it from a critique of Croce into one of Bukharin, to demonstrate Gramsci's hostility to Soviet Marxism in the time of Stalin.

14  Leading contributions include: *L'ultima ricerca di Paolo Spriano*, Rome 1988; Aldo Natoli, *Antigone e il prigionero*, Rome 1991; Giuseppe Fiori, *Gramsci, Togliatti, Stalin*, Rome 1991; Massimo Caprara, *Gramsci e i suoi carcerieri*, Milan 2001; Angelo Rossi, *Gramsci da eretico a icona*, Naples 2010; Luciano Canfora, *Gramsci in carcere e il fascismo*, Rome-Salerno 2012; Giuseppe Vacca, *Vita e pensieri di Antonio Gramsci, 1926–1937*, Turin 2012; Franco Lo Piparo, *I due carceri di Gramsci*, Rome 2012 and idem *L'enigma del quaderno*, Rome 2013; Mauro Canali, *Il tradimento*, Venice 2013. In a different category is Gerratana's edition of Sraffa's correspondence with Tatiana Schucht, *Lettere a Tania per Gramsci*, Rome 1991.

party has been, politically speaking, a *chien crevé*. Conversely, post-communism has bent every effort to defend its transformation by presenting a new image of Gramsci as not just foreshadowing, but actually already embodying the peace it has made with capitalism in general, and the American world order in particular.[15] Sensation, speculation, and manipulation have marked treatments on both sides. The most extravagant constructions, culminating in claims that Gramsci was a liberal democrat who broke with communism in prison, that Togliatti not only connived at his continued imprisonment, but after his death suppressed or destroyed a missing notebook that no doubt recorded his conversion to Western values, have come from the anti-communist side, provoking in reply a questionnaire assembling some twenty indignant or dismissive post-communist responses.[16] The furore, played out in the media, is no advertisement for the present state of intellectual life in Italy.

Abroad, the most substantial study of the *Prison Notebooks* to appear in recent years has been Peter Thomas's work *The Gramscian Moment*, which came out in 2009. Nearly half

---

15  For examples, see *The H-Word*, pp. 80–1.

16  Angelo d'Orsi (ed), *Inchiesta su Gramsci. Quaderni scomparsi, abiure, conversioni, tradimenti; leggenda o verità?*, Turin 2014. The term 'post-communist' generically describes membership of the PCI in the time when it still existed. In the great majority of cases, it has also come to mean abandonment of any connexion with communism. But in this volume, as elsewhere, there is a scattering of those who remain faithful to ideals of the past, and averse to what the Democratic Party—supposedly an heir of the PCI—has made of these. Often they come from Rifondazione comunista, the now small formation which resisted the self-dissolution of the PCI in 1991: Raul Mordenti is a notable example in this collection. A grotesque feature of much of the anti-communist literature is the claim that it represents a form of history derived from Carlo Ginzburg's recommendation of clues as a heuristic principle. From the opposite camp, Francioni had coquetted with the same conceit: *L'officina gramsciana*, p. 23.

of this is devoted to refutation of 'Antinomies', along lines inspired by Francioni, and following him, the authority of Buci-Glucksmann.[17] The centrepiece of the exercise is once more the argument, that Gramsci's variant usages of 'state' and 'civil society' are perfectly consistent with each other, derived from an 'integral' conception of the state including both. Thomas traces such an understanding of the state back to Hegel, and argues that in his development of this notion—not in his concern with hegemony—lay Gramsci's real originality. For Anglophone readers, *The Gramscian Moment* thus performs the service of introducing what Thomas describes as the philological acquisitions of 'the most recent season of Gramscian scholarship' on an expanded scale.[18] There is, it is true, an element of oddity in the performance. Motivating the length of his critique of 'Antinomies', Thomas maintains that 'it is the most well-known and influential of all studies of Gramsci in English', which 'won wide assent' as 'representative of a more general received image of Gramsci', acting indeed as a veritable 'touchstone' in the field.[19] The most cursory glance at the extant literature, overwhelmingly dominated by approaches close in spirit to that of Thomas himself, suffices to dispel any such idea.

---

17 'Anderson's error, as Francioni has demonstrated ...', 'Francioni has provided the following useful commentary ...', 'As Francioni notes ...', 'As Francioni has argued ...', 'Francioni's demonstration ...'; 'Buci-Glucksmann's *Gramsci and the State* can be read as an almost point-by-point implicit refutation of Anderson's arguments ...', 'As Buci-Glucksmann emphasises ...', 'Modifying a phrase from Buci-Glucksmann ...', 'As originally proposed by Buci-Glucksmann ...', 'As presciently noted by Buci-Glucksmann ...', 'As Buci-Glucksmann argues ...', 'As Buci-Glucksmann notes ...': *The Gramscian Moment. Philosophy, Hegemony and Marxism*, Leiden 2009, pp. 57, 81, 97, 116, 140, 220–1, 224, 238, 406.

18 *The Gramscian Moment* p. 441.

19 Ibid., pp. xx–xxi, 47, 80.

More significant than this quirk is the apolitical cast of a work whose declared aim is to 'repropose a distinctively Marxist philosophical research programme'.[20] Across four hundred and fifty pages on Gramsci, there is scarcely one concrete reference to what is known of his politics, let alone to the politics of his reception, in Italy or elsewhere—not a single mention of Athos Lisa's report on Gramsci's political lectures in prison, inconvenient from so many points of view. Though in this too following in the footsteps of Francioni, the reasons for such silence are plainly not the same, since Thomas is above suspicion of any sympathy with the Historic Compromise, or what preceded and followed it. What might explain it? The answer, in all probability, lies in dependence on the milieu of post-communist scholars in Italy whose labours *The Gramscian Moment* extols, and whose sensibilities any more robust or explicit political standpoint would offend.[21] It would be a mistake, however, to narrow this tacit connexion to a mere question of *politesse*. A shared premise is visibly at work, one that is widespread in intellectual history at large, beyond the study of Gramsci. This is the assumption—so common as to be virtually automatic—that the thought of any great mind must be as coherent as it is august, and that the highest task of commentary on it is to demonstrate its fundamental underlying unity. The reality is just the opposite: the thought of a genuinely original mind will typically exhibit—not randomly but intelligibly—significant structural contradictions, inseparable from its creativity, on which attempts to impose or extract an artificial homogeneity can only end in simplification

---

20  Ibid., p. 441.

21  Typical of the way politics features—or fails to—in the book are such formulae as: 'It is not our task here to pass judgment on the complex political calculations that prompted Togliatti …'; 'Gramsci criticises what he sees, whether fairly or not …' etc.: *The Gramscian Moment*, pp. 105–6, 213.

and distortion. Conspicuous examples are the fate of three of the most powerful political thinkers of the early modern period, Machiavelli, Hobbes and Rousseau, all of whose oeuvres are riven by central contradictions, each regularly victim of misguided efforts to apply Davidson's principle of charity to them. In the grip of this eminently conventional assumption, the aim of any well-meaning study of Gramsci becomes a demonstration of its higher unity, producing more or less ingenious exercises in what ancient and mediaeval wisdom termed 'saving the appearances'.[22] Thomas's book is not to be especially blamed for an error that is so general, nor reduced to it, since the better part of the work is concerned with the more strictly philosophical side of the *Prison Notebooks*.

In the case of Gramsci, there is an obvious contrast between what Gramsci himself believed and what became standard usages of his texts. Setting aside the record of manipulations by officialdom, this was not purely a product of distortion by subsequent interpreters. It was possible because Gramsci's intellectual explorations contain many divergent emphases, which he was under little pressure to reconcile or summarise. They do not aim at the construction of a system: there is an evident lack of anxiety about the chance of contradictions, as well as a series of circumlocutions and omissions due to censorship. Moreover, within the form of jotted enquiry that he chose, it is clear that what mainly interested Gramsci was terrain uncharted by historical materialism—questions that the Marxist tradition had said little about, taking much of what it did say for granted. The result of these two circumstances—the unbinding character of the mosaic, exploratory form, and the unspoken nature of certain

---

22 Simplicius's sixth-century term for the adjustments of Ptolemaic astronomy to anomalies in the heavens, famously at issue in the fate of Galileo.

background assumptions—was a composition that dispenses with criteria of expository coherence and protocols of reference to the Comintern canon. If Gramsci had ever been able to work the materials of the *Quaderni* up for publication, he would certainly have attended to these. We can say this with confidence from his pre-prison writings alone. The form, not unlike that of a commonplace book, that Gramsci's reflections took in prison rendered it quite possible to develop ideas in not always consistent directions, sometimes leaving a logical route to conclusions at variance with what we know on other grounds he believed. To say, as I did, that on such occasions Gramsci 'lost his way', was overly dramatic, in keeping with a rhetorical strand in the text as a whole. But that Gramsci himself was well aware of the provisional and potentially fallible character of his reflections is clear. As he wrote: 'The notes contained in this notebook, as in the others, were jotted down as quick prompts *pro memoria*. They are all to be punctiliously revised and checked, since they certainly contain imprecisions, false connexions, anachronisms. Written without access to books to which they refer, it is possible that after checking, they should be radically corrected, as the very opposite of what they say proves true.'[23]

That my essay was open to a different sort of criticism became clear to me on reading Eric Hobsbawm's reflections on Gramsci, a few months after 'Antinomies' appeared in NLR. In March 1977 he gave a short paper to a conference on Gramsci in London, published in *Marxism Today* in July, which he expanded into an address to the large fortieth anniversary conference organised by the PCI in Florence in December, subsequently published in 1982.[24] A quarter of a century later, the initial London version

---

23 *Quaderni del carcere*, II, Turin 1975, p. 1365.
24 London version—'Gramsci and Political Theory', *Marxism Today*, July

became a chapter in his collection of writings on Marxism, *How to Change the World*, which appeared in 2011.[25] But the more developed version delivered in Florence remains essential reading. In either variant, within the space of scarcely more than a dozen pages, Hobsbawm produced the best general characterisation of Gramsci as a revolutionary thinker that has yet been written, at a succinct depth without equal in the literature.

Gramsci's key originality, he argued, lay in the way in which he theorised problems both of revolutionary strategy for the conquest of power from capital, and of the construction of a society beyond capital, in a common conceptual framework based on his idea of hegemony. It was a mistake to stress only the first, without giving due weight to the second. Gramsci was fond of military metaphors, but never a prisoner of them, since 'for a soldier war is not peace, even if it is the continuation of politics by other means and victory is, professionally speaking, an end in itself', whereas for Gramsci 'the struggle to overthrow capitalism and build socialism is essentially a continuum, in which the actual transfer of power is only one moment'.[26] It followed

---

1977, pp. 205–13; Florence version—'Gramsci and Marxist Political Theory', in Anne Showstack Sassoon (ed), *Approaches to Gramsci*, London 1982, pp. 19–36; original in *Politica e storia in Gramsci*, II, Rome 1977, pp. 37–51.

25  'Gramsci', in *How to Change the World: Tales of Marx and Marxism*, London 2011, pp. 314–33. Mysteriously—a lapse of memory?—Hobsbawm sourced this chapter to the Florentine address, and listed it as previously unpublished. The variance between the two versions was a function of the audience. Listeners in London needed an explanation of the particularities of Italy that rendered a thinker like Gramsci possible, unnecessary in Italy, while listeners in Italy were entitled to more reconstruction of the political background of the Second International and of Marxist arguments at large which Gramsci confronted. Remarkably, neither version earns so much as a mention by Thomas, whose copious bibliography finds room for items by Nietzsche and Wittgenstein.

26  Florence version, p. 28.

that 'the basic problem of hegemony is not *how* revolutionaries
come to power, though this question is very important. It is
how they come to be accepted, not only as the politically existing and unavoidable rulers, but as guides and leaders'.[27] Here it
was important to remember that unlike either Marx or Lenin,
Gramsci had in post-war Turin direct experience of work in a
mass labour movement and what it meant to lead one, which
gave him a much greater sense of the cultural transformations
required, absent international war, to overturn the existing order
and to build a new society that would last. Socialism meant not
just socialisation of production, fundamental though that was,
but socialisation in the sociological sense of the word, of people
into new human relationships and structures of genuinely
popular rule, dissolving the barriers between state and civil
society. The hegemony that had to be won not just before and
during, but after a revolution, could only be achieved by active
mass participation and consensual education, 'the school of a
new consciousness, a fuller humanity for the socialist future'.[28]
In Russia, the dangers of a bureaucratism crushing any such
prospect were plainly one of his preoccupations in prison.

This was a vision, Hobsbawm remarked, based on a general
theory of politics of a kind that Marxism had always lacked,
linking Gramsci to Machiavelli as thinkers of the foundation and
transformation of societies. Distinctive of Gramsci's conception,
however, was his understanding that there is more to politics
than power—that societies are not just structures of economic
domination or political force, but possess a certain cultural
cohesion even when riven by class antagonisms. In modern
conditions, that meant the nation was always a critical arena of

27  London version, p. 211; *How to Change the World*, p. 328.
28  Florence version, p. 34.

struggles between classes. Typically, identification of the nation with the state and civil society of the rulers was the strongest element in their hegemony, and successful challenges to it a characteristic achievement of a victorious revolution.

Strategically, a war of position had been imposed on the working class in Europe in the wake of its defeats after the First World War and the isolation of the Soviet Union. But it was no absolute principle, a war of movement remaining open if circumstances changed. Nor, on the other hand, was it simply a temporary requirement in the West, but rather a necessary component of any hard revolutionary fight, everywhere in the world. Gramsci was neither any sort of gradualist nor a Eurocommunist *ante diem*, Hobsbawm told his Italian listeners. In prison, he was writing in a period of bitter working class defeats by fascism in Central and Eastern Europe, and seeking a way out of the impasse of the Third International at the time. But unlike any of its other leaders, he saw that defeat did not leave victors and vanquished unchanged, and 'might produce a much more dangerous long-term weakening of the forces of progress, by means of what he called a "passive revolution". On the one hand, the ruling class might grant certain demands to forestall and avoid revolution, on the other, the revolutionary movement might find itself in practice (though not necessarily in theory) accepting its impotence and might be eroded and politically integrated into the system'.[29] Pointed words, spoken in London, which Hobsbawm spared his audience in Florence.

Gramsci was not to be judged against present or past policies of the post-war PCI. Nor was he to be taken as an unquestioned authority. His observations on the Soviet regime in the time of Stalin were overly optimistic, and the remedies against it at

---

29  London version, p. 210; *How to Change the World*, p. 327.

which he hinted undoubtedly insufficient. The importance he attached to the role of intellectuals in the workers' movement and in history at large was not, as it stood, really convincing. To express such disagreements was to follow the example he set. Hobsbawm ended his address in Florence: 'We are fortunate enough to be able to continue his labours. I hope we shall do so with as much independence as he did'.[30]

No more compelling overview of Gramsci's thought in prison has been written. At its altitude, textual scrutiny of any detail was supernumerary. 'Antinomies' moved at a much closer level to the *Prison Notebooks*, with a more limited focus: essentially, the ways in which 'hegemony' functions in them, and its inter-connexions with the task Gramsci set himself of developing a strategy for revolution in the West, as distinct from that which had been successful in Russia. To understand these, it argued, a purely internal reconstruction of his concepts was not enough: they had to be situated in a lattice of intense debates within and beyond the international revolutionary movement of the time, which had not been looked at before. No claim was made that this line of enquiry exhausted Gramsci's intellectual or political importance. His larger conception of politics, of the nation, of intellectuals, of passive revolution—all topics touched on by Hobsbawm—as of Americanism and Fordism, not to speak of philosophy, common sense, popular culture and much else besides, lay outside its brief; their absence was no reproach to it. Exclusion of the problem of stabilizing a post-revolutionary regime was another matter. That was certainly to abridge in a quite fundamental way Gramsci's understanding of, and preoc-cupation with, hegemony. In London, Hobsbawm observed: 'we are talking here about two *different* sets of problems: strategy and

---

30  Florence version, pp. 35–6.

the nature of socialist society. Gramsci tried to get to grips with both, though some commentators [adding in Florence, 'abroad'] seem to me to have concentrated excessively on only one of them, namely the strategic.'[31] Given the lack at that date of any serious critical analysis of Gramsci's strategic thinking, it would have been difficult to measure an excess of it. But one-sided the focus of 'Antinomies' was, and remains. Hobsbawm's tacit rebuke was justified, and his reminder of the centrality for Gramsci of post-revolutionary issues a necessary corrective. In Italy, it was Sebastiano Timpanaro who made the same observation to me when it appeared there.

My explanation of the apparent casualness of Gramsci's treatment of the problematic of *Niederwerfung* in his notebooks —that he just took the principle of an 'overthrow' for granted, given its centrality to the formation of the Third International, and so of the detachment of it which he had led, and was anyway not something on which he could dwell under the eye of the censor in prison—was thus insufficient. For while Gramsci took the overthrow of the capitalist state to be indispensable, and conceived it quite classically, there was also a sense in which he thought that the construction of a revolutionary bloc before the conquest of power, and the consolidation of a new communist order after it, were harder and deeper tasks. From quite early on, he seems to have arrived at this conviction, derived in part from

---

31  London version, p. 208; *How to Change the World*, pp. 320–1, where there is one direct reference to myself, as having reminded readers of Gramsci's debt to debates in the Comintern; another, criticizing my treatment of the idea of a war of position, is dropped in his republication of the talk. Though certainly reserved about 'Antinomies'—political differences aside, close textual analysis was not his cup of tea—he did not resent application of its procedures to his own work. Years later, of an essay I had written on his autobiography and tetralogy, he said with a smile: 'You've deconstructed me, like Gramsci'.

the rapid collapse of the Hungarian and Bavarian Communes in
1919, which led him to reflect how much easier was the apparent
destruction of an older order than the effective construction of
a new one; in part from his contempt for the incendiary rhetoric of Italian Maximalists, 'who inserted the noun "violence"
between every third word in their speeches', and thought that
revolutionary;[32] and later, of course, in large part from his
concern for the fate of the *smychka*—the alliance of workers and
peasants—in Russia, and more generally the direction that party
rule was taking after the death of Lenin. Guarding against these
dangers, the principle of hegemony was the connective tissue
capable of unifying the revolutionary process across the divide
between opposite social orders and political regimes.

There I overlooked what Gerratana, alone in his party, had
seen in the seventies. Under pressure from the PSI symposium
in *Mondoperaio*, the PCI organised its own seminar on Gramsci
in early 1977, at which he delivered the sole distinguished contribution, that would subsequently appear in modified form in
the papers for the conference at Florence, and a decade later
be distilled into the finest concentrate of Gramsci's conception of hegemony, at a level textually closer than that offered
by Hobsbawm, that we possess.[33] Linking two passages in the
*Notebooks*, Gerratana pointed out that a structural distinction
between bourgeois and proletarian hegemony—which I had
argued was missing in Gramsci—could in fact be found in them.
In the first, Gramsci not only illustrated his famous contrast

32 'La guerra è la guerra', *Socialismo e fascismo. L'Ordine Nuovo 1921–1922*,
Turin 1966, p. 58.
33 Respectively: 'Stato, partito, strumenti e istituti dell'egemonia nei "Quaderni del carcere"', in *Egemonia Stato partito in Gramsci*, pp. 37–53; 'Gramsci
come pensatore rivoluzionario', in *Politica e Storia in Gramsci*, II, pp. 69–99,
and 'Le forme dell'egemonia' in *Gramsci. Problemi di metodo*, pp. 119–26.

between domination and direction, the one directed at adversaries and the other at allies, and the possibility of the second preceding the first, with the example of the hegemony of the Moderates over the Action Party in the Risorgimento, but went on to observe that after the unification of Italy was achieved, the Moderates continued to exercise a hegemony whose parliamentary expression was *trasformismo*—'that is, the development of an ever broader ruling class' by 'gradual but continual absorption, with methods of variable efficacy, of the active elements of allied groups and even of adversaries who seemed irreconcilable enemies. In this sense political direction became an aspect of the function of domination, in so far as the absorption of the elites of enemy groups led to their decapitation and annihilation for a period that was often very long'.[34] Bourgeois hegemony, in other words, extended beyond allies to adversaries, direction becoming subsumed in domination.

Could proletarian hegemony reproduce this figure of power? It could not, Gerratana argued, for a reason indicated by Gramsci elsewhere. Bourgeois ideologies were designed to mask contradictory interests by offering the appearance of a peaceful reconciliation of them, concealing the exploitation on which the society of capital was based. They required deception. Marxism, by contrast, was the exposure of the contradiction between capital and labour on which bourgeois civilisation rested, and demanded the truth about both. For it was 'not an instrument of the rule of dominant groups to obtain consensus and exercise hegemony over subaltern classes', but 'an expression of these subaltern classes which want to educate themselves in the art of government and whose interest is in knowing all the truth, even when it is harsh, and avoiding not only the

34 *Quaderni del carcere*, III, p. 2011.

(impossible) deceptions of the class above it, but still more any self-deceptions'.[35] This was a fundamental difference. It was taken for granted by the established order that 'lying is essential to the art of politics, the astute ability to conceal one's real opinions and aims, to give out the opposite of what one wants', but 'in mass politics, to speak the truth is a precise political necessity', and the kinds of consent on which each form of hegemony rested were consequently opposites: 'passive and indirect' subordination in one case, 'direct and active participation' in the other.[36]

The difference at work in these passages is, in effect, deontological—what in the Crocean terms adopted on occasion by Gramsci could be called ethico-political. They speak of what the hegemony of the working class should be, without raising the empirical question of what, on a realistic historical reckoning, it could be. There, Gramsci had an answer in the time of the factory councils in Turin, when not for nothing was his paper entitled *L'Ordine Nuovo*. The test of proletarian hegemony was its ability to unleash productive superior forces, by not only occupying but operating industrial plants, after banishing managers and capitalists from them. 'Two Revolutions', written in July 1920 between the peaks of labour insurgency in Northern Italy, April and September of that year, was explicit: if the revolution had failed in Germany, Austria, Bavaria, the Ukraine and Hungary, it was because 'the presence of external conditions—a communist party, the destruction of the bourgeois state, highly organised trade-unions and an armed proletariat—was not enough to compensate for the absence of another condition'—'a conscious movement of the proletarian masses to give substance to their political power with economic power, and a determination on

---

35   *Quaderni del carcere*, II, p. 1319.
36   Ibid., II, pp. 699–700, III, p. 1771.

the part of these proletarian masses to introduce proletarian order into the factory, to make the factory the nucleus of the new state.' [37]

In the *Prison Notebooks*, Gramsci continued to express a belief that the hegemony of the proletariat had to be anchored in production, but the essential emphasis of his conception of it had shifted. Hegemony, now repeatedly associated with superstructures, became preeminently a matter of cultural ascendancy. Could the working class hope to exercise that before it won power, as the bourgeoisie had done before it? The standard readings of Gramsci in Italy and elsewhere held that this was his suggestion. There is no doubt that many of his entries left such a construction of them open, and such was my criticism of them. But his notes contain counter-indications, the most important of which I noted, even if these still sit awkwardly amid the general direction of his comments, an example of the discrepancies inseparable from their form. Twice, the same adverb delivers the necessary rectification: 'subaltern groups always undergo the initiative of dominant groups, even when they rise up and rebel: only "permanent" victory breaks, and not immediately, their subordination'—'only after the creation of the state is the cultural problem posed in all its complexity and tends towards a coherent solution.' [38]

Gerratana, the one cogent critic of Salvadori from the PCI in 1977, made no secret of his disagreement with party notables

---

37 'Due rivoluzioni', in *L'Ordine Nuovo 1919–1920*, Turin 1987, pp. 569–71—a fundamental text for his thought as a whole.

38 *Quaderni del carcere*, III, pp. 2283–4, p. 1863. The passage to which I drew attention in 'Antinomies' ascribed 'statolatry' in Soviet Russia to the proletariat's lack of any 'long period of independent cultural and moral development, capable of creating a civil society of its own, before the conquest of power.' See below, pp. 100, 114.

who were already calling on it to 'go beyond' hegemony, arguing firmly for the need to remain faithful to 'the general project of a social transformation of universal character', rather than a mere reformism 'satisfied with itself'.[39] Gramsci was a revolutionary thinker, he reminded those in attendance at Florence capable of forgetting it. His final thoughts on hegemony were delivered in Moscow in 1987, on the eve of the end of the Soviet experience.

*

In the years since, the twin problematics that were central to Gramsci in his lifetime—the overcoming of capitalism, the building of socialism—have faded from the horizon. Forces of production have not burst relations of production; the labour movement is a shadow of its past; mourned or execrated, the October Revolution is a distant memory.

In the conjuncture of 'Antinomies'—this was as true of Hobsbawm or Gerratana as of myself—we were writing of a different era: a time when there had recently been the largest mass strike in history in France, the overthrow of a government by workers in Britain, continuous outbreaks of revolt in Italy, the defeat of the United States in Vietnam, and a revolution in Portugal, where hopes and fears of a social upheaval, galvanizing Washington and Bonn to vigilance, were still fresh. It was the last hour of what Lukács, in his tribute to Lenin in 1923, had called the actuality of the revolution. Portugal features both in 'Antinomies' and in Hobsbawm's rejoinders to it. On reading the first, Franco Moretti told me, as I have written elsewhere, that it was a fitting

---

39  See his contributions in the debate at the end of *Egemonia e democrazia*, pp. 211, 216.

farewell to the revolutionary Marxist tradition.[40] That was not how I saw it then. But time was on his side, where it has remained.

It was a contemporary and, in those years, friend of his, Galli della Loggia, who saw more clearly than anyone else in 1976–7 what lay ahead. Though opposite in their depictions of Gramsci, he remarked, both sides in the debate set off by Salvadori had missed his real significance, failing to understand that his conception of hegemony was not just a political, but an epochal category. It designated the *Weltanschauung* of an entire society, as Hegel had conceived their succession from one spirit of the age to the next, exemplified in modern times by the encompassing ideology of bourgeois society in Europe at its height, which Gramsci believed would be followed by the sway of a comparable *Weltanschauung*—the 'philosophy of praxis'—to come.

But the society to which industrial capitalism had given birth had no place for ideologies of this kind. Hegemony in it could dispense with them; it lay in a set of lifestyles, conducts, needs, demands, whose origin and end was in the world of commodities—their production, consumption and distribution. Mass industrial democracy had no ethos, no directive idea, no concern with the inner life of the individual, which was delivered over to the market and the unconscious. Intellectuals, to whom Gramsci attached such importance, were either entirely detached from this universe or utterly immersed in it, vectors of high and low culture that could no longer generate any synthesis. Its basic value was tolerance, that is, indifference. Because Italy was still a relatively backward capitalist society in Gramsci's time, he could think the Hegelian vision might continue. He was too Italian, too Southern, to understand that 'his' Croce, 'his' Vatican, 'his' peasants, 'his' intellectuals—all the national furniture of his

---

40  *A Zone of Engagement*, London-New York 1992, p. xi.

mind—were about to vanish. The new hegemony would rival in strength that of any in history. But it would be anthropological, not ideological. Was it stable? Based on the desires of the individual, it could only lead to an acute crisis of individuality, whose symptoms could already be detected in the school and the family. Bobbio was right: democracy was a road that led no-one knew where. But it was absurd to pretend nothing had changed.[41]

The overstatement in this verdict was, no doubt, itself ideological enough. But that it captured features of the postmodern landscape of capital that would emerge within a few years, and is still with us, is incontestable. The passionate world of ideas and arguments explored below belongs, as Galli della Loggia saw, to another epoch. That is true, of course, of all significant political debates of the past, few failing to repay historical enquiry altogether. How far this particular past is only of antiquarian, rather than contemporary, interest is less clear. If capital has seen off any prospect of revolution in the West, for some time now it has also dealt a quietus to what was traditionally its alternative. 'Reforms', since the eighties, have typically come to mean the introduction not of milder but harsher forms of capitalism, not less but more ruthless styles of exploitation and neglect. In that neoliberal inversion, the recent fate of social democracy is written. Viewed world-historically, the difference it has made has not been great. The welfare state attributed to it exists in countries where it has never enjoyed significant power—Japan, Switzerland, Ireland, Canada, even in its fashion the United States—as well as those in which it has. In favourable conditions, it has yielded a set of small societies in Scandinavia markedly more civilised than the

---

41 'Le ceneri di Gramsci', *Egemonia e democrazia*, pp. 69–91, its title taken from Pasolini's poem of 1957. Today the author is a leading editorialist in the *Corriere della sera*.

bourgeois median, even if these too are now subject to erosion. The balance sheet of what was once reformism is not negligible, but it is modest. Of the revolutionary tradition, that cannot be said. Europe was largely saved from Nazism by the Red Army, and China today looms larger in the scales of growth and power than the Soviet Union ever did. The crimes and disasters, not to speak of the ironies and reversals, of the communist record are plain. But that it changed the world as the Second International never did is equally plain. Not coincidentally, the legacy of its ideas, for those with any interest in ideas, is much richer. Gramsci alone is sufficient testimony to that.

*

*The Antinomies of Antonio Gramsci* appears together with a companion study, *The H-Word*, which as I explain there, germinated from it. There is an overlap between the two, some findings in this essay requiring a brief rehearsal in its pendant, which readers coming upon both must excuse. In the interests of readability, I have lightened the text of some, though not all, of its excess verbal baggage—rhetoric of the period—but otherwise left as it stands, arguments unaltered. In an annexe, I have included for the first time in English the report on Gramsci in prison written by his fellow prisoner Athos Lisa, without which no historically truthful account of his political outlook at the time is possible. Finally, I should mention what in some respects can be regarded a sequel, 'The Heirs of Gramsci', published in No. 100 of the second series of *New Left Review*, as 'The Antinomies of Antonio Gramsci' was in No. 100 of the first. I have drawn on its opening paragraphs for this preface. The rest can be found in *The H-Word*, save for its conclusion.

*October 2016*

# THE ANTINOMIES OF
# ANTONIO GRAMSCI

# 1

# ALTERATION

No Marxist thinker after the classical epoch is so generally respected in the West as Antonio Gramsci. Nor is any term so freely or diversely invoked on the left as that of hegemony, to which he gave currency. Gramsci's reputation, still local and marginal outside his native Italy in the early sixties, has a decade later become a worldwide fame. The homage due to his enterprise in prison is now—thirty years after the first publication of his notebooks—finally and fully being paid. Lack of knowledge, or paucity of discussion, have ceased to be obstacles to the diffusion of his thought. In principle every revolutionary socialist, not only in the West—if especially in the West—can henceforward benefit from Gramsci's patrimony. Yet at the same time, the spread of Gramsci's renown has not to date been accompanied by any corresponding depth of enquiry into his work. The very range of the appeals now made to his authority, from the most contrasted sectors of the left, suggests the limits of close study or comprehension of his ideas. The price of so ecumenical an admiration is necessarily ambiguity: multiple and incompatible interpretations of the themes of the *Prison Notebooks*.

There are, of course, good reasons for this. No Marxist work is so difficult to read accurately and systematically, because of the peculiar conditions of its composition. To start with, Gramsci underwent the normal fate of original theorists, from which neither Marx nor Lenin was exempt: the necessity of working towards radically new concepts in an old vocabulary, designed for other purposes and times, which overlaid and deflected their meaning. Just as Marx had to think many of his innovations in the language of Hegel or Smith, Lenin in that of Plekhanov and Kautsky, so Gramsci often had to produce his concepts within the archaic and inadequate apparatus of Croce or Machiavelli. This familiar problem, however, is compounded by the fact that Gramsci wrote in prison, under atrocious conditions, with a fascist censor scrutinizing everything that he produced. The involuntary disguise that inherited language so often imposes on a pioneer was thus superimposed by a voluntary one which Gramsci assumed to evade his jailers. The result is a work censored twice over: its spaces, ellipses, contradictions, disorders, allusions, repetitions, are the result of this uniquely adverse process of composition. The reconstruction of the hidden order within these hieroglyphs remains to be done. This difficult enterprise has scarcely yet been started. A systematic work of recovery is needed to discover what Gramsci wrote in the true, obliterated text of his thought. It is necessary to say this as a warning against all facile or complacent readings of Gramsci: he is still largely an unknown author to us.

It has now become urgent, however, to look again, soberly and comparatively, at the texts that have made Gramsci most famous. For the great mass Communist Parties of Western Europe—in Italy, in France, in Spain—are now on the threshold of a historical experience without precedent for them: the assumption of governmental office within the framework of bourgeois-democratic states, without the allegiance to a horizon of 'proletarian dictatorship' beyond them that was once the touchstone of the Third International. If one political ancestry is more widely and insistently invoked than any other for the new perspectives of 'Eurocommunism', it is that of Gramsci. It is not necessary to accredit any apocalyptic vision of the immediate future to sense the significance of the approaching tests for the history of the working class throughout Western Europe. The present political conjuncture calls for a serious and responsible clarification of the themes in Gramsci's work which are now commonly associated with the new design of Latin communism.

At the same time, of course, Gramsci's influence is by no means confined to those countries where there exist major Communist Parties, poised for entry into government. The adoption of concepts from the *Prison Notebooks* has, in fact, been especially marked in the theoretical and historical work of the British left in recent years, and to a lesser extent of the American left. The sudden phenomenon of very widespread borrowing from Gramsci within Anglo-Saxon political culture provides a second, more parochial prompting to re-examine his legacy in these pages. For *New Left Review* was the first socialist journal in Britain—possibly the first anywhere outside Italy—to make deliberate and systematic use of Gramsci's theoretical canon to analyse its own national society, and to debate a political strategy capable of transforming it. The essays that sought to realise this project were published in 1964–5.[1] At the time, Gramsci's work

---

1  See Tom Nairn, 'The British Political Elite', *New Left Review* 23, January–February 1964; Perry Anderson, 'Origins of the Present Crisis', ibid.; Nairn, 'The English Working Class', *New Left Review* 24, March–April 1964; Nairn, 'The Nature of the Labour Party', *New Left Review* 27 and 28, September–October and November–December 1964; Anderson, 'The Left in the Fifties', *New Left Review* 29, January-February 1965; Nairn, 'Labour Imperialism',

was unfamiliar in England: the articles in question were gener-ally contested.[2] By 1973–5, Gramscian themes and notions of a similar tenor were ubiquitous. In particular, the central concept of 'hegemony', first utilised as the leitmotif of the NLR theses of the early sixties, has since enjoyed an exceptional fortune. Historians, literary critics, philosophers, economists and politi-cal scientists have employed it with ever-increasing frequency.[3] Amidst the profusion of usages and allusions, however, there has been relatively little inspection of the actual texts in which Gramsci developed his theory of hegemony. A more direct and exact reflection on these is now overdue.

The purpose of this essay, then, will be to analyse the forms and functions of Gramsci's concept of hegemony in his *Prison Notebooks*, and to assess their internal coherence as a unified discourse; to consider their validity as an account of the typical structures of class power in the bourgeois democracies of the West; and finally to weigh their strategic consequences for the struggle of the working class to achieve emancipation and social-ism. Its procedure will of necessity be primarily philological:

---

*New Left Review* 32, July–August 1965. Further developments of the theses on English history and society contained in these initial essays included: Anderson, 'Socialism and Pseudo-Empiricism', *New Left Review* 35, January–February 1966; Anderson, 'Components of the National Culture', *New Left Review* 50, July-August 1968; Nairn, 'The Fateful Meridian', *New Left Review* 60, March–April 1970.

2   The major response was the famous essay by Edward Thompson, 'The Peculiarities of the English', *The Socialist Register 1965*. Its criticisms prob-ably won general assent on the British left.

3   Among the most notable examples of creative use of Gramsci's concept in recent works are: Eric Hobsbawm, *The Age of Capital*, London 1975, pp. 249–50; Edward Thompson, *Whigs and Hunters*, London 1975, pp. 262, 269; Raymond Williams, 'Base and Superstructure', *NLR* 82, November-December 1973—reworked in *Marxism and Literature*, London 1977; Eugene Genovese, *Roll, Jordan, Roll*, New York 1974, pp. 25–8.

an attempt to fix with greater precision what Gramsci said and meant in his captivity; to locate the sources from which he derived the terms of his discourse; and to reconstruct the network of oppositions and correspondences in the thought of his contemporaries into which his writing was inserted—in other words, the true theoretical context of his work. These formal enquiries are the indispensable condition, it will be argued, of any substantive judgement of Gramsci's theory of hegemony.

We may begin by recalling the most celebrated passages of all in the *Prison Notebooks*—the legendary fragments in which Gramsci contrasted the political structures of 'East' and 'West', and the revolutionary strategies pertinent to each of them. These texts represent the most cogent synthesis of the essential terms of Gramsci's theoretical universe, which elsewhere are dispersed and scattered throughout the notebooks. They do not immediately broach the problem of hegemony. However, they assemble all the necessary elements for its emergence into a controlling position in his discourse. The two central notes focus on the relationship between state and civil society, in Russia and in Western Europe respectively.[4] In each case, they do so by way of the same military analogy.

---

4   All references to Gramsci's work will be to the *Critical Edition* edited by Valentino Gerratana: Antonio Gramsci, *Quaderni del Carcere*, Turin 1975, I–IV. Volumes I–III present for the first time the complete and exact texts of the notebooks, in their order of composition; Volume IV contains the critical apparatus assembled by Gerratana, with admirable care and discretion. The edition as a whole is a model of scholarly scruple and clarity. Wherever the texts cited in this essay are included in the English collection, *Selections from the Prison Notebooks*, edited by Quintin Hoare and Geoffrey Nowell-Smith, London 1971, references are also given to the latter, and translations are usually taken from it, with occasional modifications. The English editors provide far the best informative apparatus available to any foreign-language readership of Gramsci. Abbreviations will be *QC* and *SPN* respectively, throughout.

In the first, Gramsci discusses the rival strategies of the high commands in the First World War, and concludes that they suggest a critical lesson for class politics after the war:

General Krasnov has asserted (in his novel) that the Entente did not wish for the victory of Imperial Russia for fear that the Eastern Question would definitively be resolved in favour of Tsarism, and therefore obliged the Russian General Staff to adopt trench warfare (absurd, in view of the enormous length of the front from the Baltic to the Black Sea, with vast marshy and forest zones), whereas the only possible strategy was a war of manoeuvre. This assertion is merely silly. In actual fact, the Russian Army did attempt a war of manoeuvre and sudden incursion, especially in the Austrian sector (but also in East Prussia), and won successes as brilliant as they were ephemeral. The truth is that one cannot choose the form of war one wants, unless from the start one has a crushing superiority over the enemy. It is well known what losses were incurred by the stubborn refusal of the General Staffs to acknowledge that a war of position was 'imposed' by the overall relation of forces in conflict. A war of position is not, in reality, constituted simply by actual trenches, but by the whole organisational and industrial system of the territory which lies to the back of the army in the field. It is imposed notably by the rapid fire-power of cannons, machine-guns and rifles, by the armed strength that can be concentrated at a particular spot, as well as by the abundance of supplies that make possible the swift replacement of material lost after an enemy breakthrough or retreat. A further factor is the great mass of men under arms; they are of a very unequal calibre, and are precisely only able to operate as a mass force. It can be seen how on the Eastern Front it was one thing to make an incursion into the Austrian sector, and another into the German sector; and how even in the Austrian sector, reinforced by picked German troops and commanded by Germans, incursion tactics ended in disaster. The same thing happened in the Polish

Campaign of 1920; the seemingly irresistible advance was halted before Warsaw by General Weygand, on the line commanded by French officers. The very military experts who are believers in wars of position, just as they previously were in wars of manoeuvre, naturally do not maintain that the latter should be expunged from military science. They merely maintain that in wars among the more industrially and socially advanced States, war of manoeuvre must be considered reduced to more of a tactical than a strategic function, occupying the same position as siege warfare previously held in relation to it. The same reduction should be effected in the art and science of politics, at least in the case of the advanced States, where 'civil society' has become a very complex structure and one that is resistant to the catastrophic 'incursions' of the immediate economic element (crises, depressions, and so on). The superstructures of civil society are like the trench-systems of modern warfare. In war it would happen sometimes that a fierce artillery attack seemed to have destroyed the enemy's entire defensive system, whereas in fact it had only destroyed the outer surface of it; and at the moment of their advance and attack the assailants would find themselves con-fronted by a line of defence which was still effective. The same thing happens in politics, during the great economic crises. A crisis cannot give the attacking forces the ability to organise with lightning speed in time and space; still less can it endow them with fighting spirit. Similarly, the defenders are not demoralised, nor do they abandon their positions, even among the ruins, nor do they lose faith in their own strength or in their own future. Of course, things do not remain exactly as they were; but it is certain that one will not find the element of speed, of accelerated time, of the definitive forward march expected by the strategists of political Cadornism. The last occurrence of the kind in the history of politics was the events of 1917. They marked a decisive turning-point in the history of the art and science of politics.[5]

---

5   *QC* III, pp. 1614–6; *SPN*, pp. 234–5.

In the second text, Gramsci proceeds to a direct counterposition of the course of the Russian Revolution and the character of a correct strategy for socialism in the West, by way of a contrast between the relationship of state and civil society in the two geopolitical theatres:

It should be seen whether Trotsky's famous theory about the permanent character of the movement is not the political reflection of … the general economic-cultural-social conditions in a country in which the structures of national life are embryonic and loose, and incapable of becoming 'trench' or 'fortress'. In this case one might say that Trotsky, apparently 'Western', was in fact a cosmopolitan—that is, superficially Western or European. Lenin on the other hand was profoundly national and profoundly European … It seems to me that Lenin understood that a change was necessary from the war of manoeuvre applied victoriously in the East in 1917, to a war of position which was the only possible form in the West—where, as Krasnov observed, armies could rapidly accumulate endless quantities of munitions, and where the social structures were of themselves still capable of becoming heavily armed fortifications. This is what the formula of the 'united front' seems to me to mean, and it corresponds to the conception of a single front for the Entente under the sole command of Foch. Lenin, however, did not have time to expand his formula—though it should be remembered that he could only have expanded it theoretically, whereas the fundamental task was a national one; that is to say, it demanded a reconnaissance of the terrain and identification of the elements of trench and fortress represented by the elements of civil society, and so on. In the East, the State was everything, civil society was primordial and gelatinous; in the West, there was a proper relationship between State and civil society, and when the State trembled a sturdy structure of civil society was at once revealed. The State was only an outer ditch, behind which there was a powerful system of fortresses and earthworks: more or less numerous from one State to the next it goes without saying—but this precisely necessitated an accurate reconnaissance of each individual country.[6]

There are a number of memorable themes in these two extremely compressed and dense passages, which are echoed in other fragments of the *Notebooks*. For the moment, our intention is not to reconstitute and explore either of them, or relate them to Gramsci's thought as a whole. It will merely be enough to set out the main apparent elements of which they are composed, in a series of oppositions:

|  | East | West |
|---|---|---|
| *Civil Society* | Primordial/Gelatinous | Developed/Sturdy |
| *State* | Preponderant | Balanced |
| *Strategy* | Manoeuvre | Position |
| *Tempo* | Speed | Protraction |

While the terms of each opposition are not given any precise definition in the texts, the relations between the two sets initially appear clear and coherent enough. A closer look, however, immediately reveals certain discrepancies. Firstly, the economy is described as making 'incursions' into civil society in the West as an elemental force; the implication is evidently that it is situated outside it. Yet the normal usage of the term 'civil society' ever since Hegel had preeminently included the sphere of the economy, as that of material needs; it was in this sense that it was always employed by Marx and Engels. Here, on the contrary, it seems to exclude economic relations. At the same time, the second note contrasts the East, where the state is 'everything', with the West where the state and civil society are in a 'proper'

6    *QC* II, pp. 865–6; *SPN*, pp. 236–8.

relationship. It can be assumed, without forcing the text, that Gramsci meant by this something like a 'balanced' relationship; in a letter written a year or so before, he refers to 'an equilibrium of political society and civil society', where by political society he intended the state.[7] Yet the text goes on to say that in the war of position in the West, the state constitutes only the 'outer ditch' of civil society, which can resist its demolition. Civil society thereby becomes a central core or inner redoubt, of which the state is merely an external and dispensable surface. Is this compatible with the image of a 'balanced relationship' between the two? The contrast in the two relationships between state and civil society in East and West becomes a simple inversion here—no longer preponderance *versus* equilibrium, but one preponderance against another preponderance.

An accurate reading of these fragments is rendered even more complex when it is realised that while their formal objects of criticism are Trotsky and Luxemburg, their real target may have been the Third Period of the Comintern. We can surmise this from the date of their composition—somewhere between 1930 and 1932 in the *Notebooks*—and from the transparent reference to the Great Depression of 1929, on which many of the sectarian conceptions of 'social-fascism' during the Third Period were founded. Gramsci fought these ideas resolutely from prison, and in doing so was led to reappropriate the Comintern's political prescriptions of 1921, when Lenin was still alive, of tactical unity with all other working class parties in the struggle against capital, which he himself along with nearly every other important leader of the Italian Communist Party had rejected at the time. Hence the 'dislocated' reference to the United Front in a text which seems to speak of a quite different debate.

---

7   *Lettere dal Carcere*, Turin 1965, p. 481.

A comparison of these fragments with another crucial text from the *Notebooks* reveals even more difficulties. Gramsci alludes to the theme of 'Permanent Revolution' a number of times. The other main passage in which he refers to it is this:

The political concept of the so-called 'Permanent Revolution', which emerged before 1848 as a scientifically evolved expression of the Jacobin experience from 1789 to Thermidor, belongs to a historical period in which the great mass political parties and the economic trade unions did not yet exist, and society was still in a state of fluidity from many points of view, so to speak. There was a greater backwardness of the countryside, and virtually complete monopoly of political and State power by a few cities or even by a single one (Paris in the case of France); a relatively rudimentary State apparatus, and a greater autonomy of civil society from State activity; a specific system of military forces and national armed services; greater autonomy of the national economies from the economic relations of the world market, and so on. In the period after 1870, with the colonial expansion of Europe, all these elements change. The internal and international organisational relations of the State become more complex and massive, and the Forty-Eightist formula of the 'Permanent Revolution' is expanded and superseded in political science by the formula of the 'civil hegemony'. The same thing happens in the art of politics as in military art: war of movement increasingly becomes war of position, and it can be said that a State will win a war in so far as it prepares for it minutely and technically in peacetime. The massive structure of the modern democracies, both as State organisations and as complexes of associations in civil society, are for the art of politics what 'trenches' and permanent fortifications of the front are for the war of position. They render merely 'partial' the element of movement which used to be the 'whole' of war. This question is posed for the modern States, but not for the backward countries or for the colonies, where forms which elsewhere have been superseded and have become anachronistic are still in vigour.[8]

Here the terms of the first two fragments are recombined into a new order, and their meaning appears to shift accordingly. 'Permanent Revolution' now clearly refers to Marx's 'Address to the Communist League of 1850', when he advocated an escalation from the bourgeois revolution which had just swept Europe to a proletarian revolution. The Commune marks the end of this hope. Henceforward war of position replaces permanent revolution. The distinction East/West reappears in the form of a demarcation of 'modern democracies' from 'backward and colonial societies' where a war of movement still prevails. This change in context corresponds to a shift in the relations between 'state' and 'civil society'. In 1848, the state is 'rudimentary' and civil society is 'autonomous' from it. After 1870, the internal and international organisation of the state becomes 'complex and massive', while civil society also becomes correspondingly developed. It is now that the concept of hegemony appears. For the new strategy necessary is precisely that of 'civil hegemony'. The meaning of the latter is unexplained here; it is, however, clearly related to that of 'war of position'. What is striking in this third fragment, then, is its emphasis on the massive expansion of the Western state from the late nineteenth century onwards, with a subordinate allusion to a parallel development of civil society. There is no explicit reversal of the terms, yet the context and weight of the passage virtually imply a new prepotence of the state.

It is not difficult, in effect, to discern in Gramsci's text the echo of Marx's famous denunciation of the 'monstrous parasitic

---

8    QC III, pp. 1566–7; SPN, pp. 242–3.

machine' of the Bonapartist state in France. His periodisation is somewhat different from that of Marx, since he dates the change from the victory of Thiers and not that of Louis Napoleon, but the theme is that of *The Eighteenth Brumaire* and *The Civil War in France*. In the former, it will be remembered, Marx wrote: 'Only under the second Bonaparte does the State seem to have attained a completely autonomous position. The State machine has established itself so firmly *vis-a-vis* civil society that the only leader it needs is the head of the Society of 10 December ... The State enmeshes, controls, regulates, supervises and regiments civil society from the most all-embracing expressions of its life down to its most insignificant motions, from its most general modes of existence down to the private life of individuals.'[9] Gramsci makes no such extreme claim. Yet, setting aside the rhetoric of Marx's account, the logic of Gramsci's text leans in the same direction, to the extent that it clearly implies that civil society has lost the 'autonomy' of the state which it once possessed.

There is thus an oscillation between at least three different 'positions' of the state in the West in these initial texts alone. It is in a 'balanced relationship' with civil society, it is only an 'outer surface' of civil society, it is the 'massive structure' which cancels the autonomy of civil society. These oscillations, moreover, concern only the relationship between the terms. The terms themselves, however, are subject to the same sudden shifts of boundary and position. In all the above quotations, the opposition is between 'state' and 'civil society'. Yet elsewhere Gramsci speaks of the state itself as inclusive of civil society, defining it thus: 'The general notion of the State includes elements which need to be referred back to the notion of civil society (in the sense that one might say that the State = political society + civil society,

9   Karl Marx, *Surveys from Exile*, London 1973, pp. 238, 186.

in other words hegemony armoured with coercion).'[10] Here
the distinction between 'political society' and 'civil society' is
maintained, while the term 'state' encompasses the two. In other
passages, however, Gramsci goes further and directly rejects any
opposition between political and civil society, as a confusion
of liberal ideology. 'The ideas of the Free Trade movement are
based on a theoretical error, whose practical origin is not hard
to identify; they are based on a distinction between political
society and civil society, which is rendered and presented as an
organic one, whereas in fact it is merely methodological. Thus
it is asserted that economic activity belongs to civil society, and
that the State must not intervene to regulate it. But since in actual
reality civil society and State are one and the same, it must be
made clear that laissez-faire too is a form of State "regulation",
introduced and maintained by legislative and coercive means.'[11]
Political society is here an express synonym for the state, and
any substantive separation of the two is denied. It is evident that
another semantic shift has occurred. In other words, the state
itself oscillates between three definitions:

| State | contrasts with | Civil Society |
| State | encompasses | Civil Society |
| State | is identical with | Civil Society |

Thus both the terms and the relations between them are subject
to sudden variations or mutations. It will be seen that these shifts
are not arbitrary or accidental. They have a determinate meaning
within the architecture of Gramsci's work. For the moment,
however, an elucidation of them can be deferred.

For there remains one further concept of Gramsci's discourse

---

10  *QC* II, pp. 763–4; *SPN*, p. 263.
11  *QC* III, pp. 1589–90; *SPN*, p. 160.

which is centrally related to the problematic of these texts. That is, of course, hegemony. The term, it will be remembered, occurs in the third passage as a strategy of 'war of position' to replace the 'war of manoeuvre' of an earlier epoch. This war of manoeuvre is identified with the 'Permanent Revolution' of Marx in 1848. In the second text, the identification reappears, but the reference here is to Trotsky in the 1920s. The 'war of position' is now attributed to Lenin and equated with the idea of the United Front. There is thus a loop:

Civil Hegemony = War of Position = United Front

The next question is therefore naturally what Gramsci meant precisely by war of position or civil hegemony. Hitherto, we have been concerned with terms whose ancestry is familiar. The notions of 'state' and 'civil society', dating from the Renaissance and the Enlightenment respectively, present no particular problems. However diverse their usage, they have long formed part of common political parlance on the left. The term 'hegemony' has no such immediate currency. In fact, Gramsci's concept in the *Prison Notebooks* is frequently believed to be an entirely novel coinage—in effect, his own invention.[12] The word might perhaps be found in stray phrases of writers before him, it is often suggested, but the concept as a theoretical unit is his creation.

Nothing reveals the lack of scholarship from which Gramsci's legacy has suffered more than this widespread illusion. For in fact the notion of hegemony had a long prior history, before Gramsci's adoption of it, that is of great significance for understanding its

---

12  See, for representative examples, Norberto Bobbio, 'Gramsci e la concezione della società civile', in the symposium *Gramsci e la Cultura Contemporanea*, Rome 1969, p. 94; and more recently, Maria-Antonietta Macciocchi, *Pour Gramsci*, Paris 1974, p. 140.

later function in his work. The term *gegemoniya* (hegemony) was one of the most central political slogans in the Russian Social-Democratic movement, from the late 1890s to 1917. The idea which it codified first started to emerge in the writings of Plekhanov in 1883–4, where he urged the need for the Russian working class to wage a political struggle against Tsarism, not merely an economic struggle against its employers. In his founding programme of the Emancipation of Labour Group in 1884, he argued that the bourgeoisie in Russia was still too weak to take the initiative in the struggle against Absolutism: the organised working class would have to take up the demands of a bourgeois-democratic revolution.[13] Plekhanov in these texts used the vague term 'domination' (*gospodstvo*) for political power as such, and continued to assume that the proletariat would support the bourgeoisie in a revolution in which the latter would necessarily emerge in the end as the leading class.[14] By 1889, his emphasis had shifted somewhat: 'political freedom' would now be 'won by the working class or not at all'—yet at the same time without challenging the ultimate domination of capital in Russia.[15] In the next decade, his colleague Axelrod went further. In two important pamphlets of 1898, polemicizing against Economism, he declared that the Russian working class could and must play an 'independent, leading role in the struggle against absolutism', for the 'political impotence of all other classes' conferred a 'central, pre-eminent importance' on the proletariat.[16] 'The vanguard of

---

13 G.V. Plekhanov, *Izbrannye Filosofskie Proizvedeniya*, I, Moscow 1956, p. 372.
14 Plekhanov, *Sochineniya*, (ed. Ryazanov), Moscow 1923, II, pp. 55, 63, 77; III, p. 91.
15 *Sochineniya*, II, p. 347.
16 P. Axelrod, *K Voprosu o Sovremennykh Zadachykh i Taktik Russkikh Sotsial-Demokratov*, Geneva 1898, pp. 20, 26.

the working class should systematically behave as the leading detachment of democracy in general.'[17] Axelrod still oscillated between ascription of an 'independent' and a 'leading' role to the proletariat, and ascribed exaggerated importance to gentry opposition to Tsarism, within what he reaffirmed would be a bourgeois revolution. However, his ever-greater emphasis on the 'all-national revolutionary significance'[18] of the Russian working class soon catalysed a qualitative theoretical change. For it was henceforward the primacy of the proletariat in the bourgeois revolution in Russia that would be unambiguously announced.

In a letter to Struve in 1901, demarcating social-democratic from liberal perspectives in Russia, Axelrod now stated as an axiom: 'By virtue of the historical position of our proletariat, Russian Social-Democracy can acquire hegemony (*gegemoniya*) in the struggle against absolutism.'[19] The younger generation of Marxist theorists adopted the concept immediately. In the same year, Martov was to write in a polemical article: 'The struggle between the "critics" and "orthodox" Marxists is really the first chapter of a struggle for political hegemony between the proletariat and bourgeois democracy.'[20] Lenin, meanwhile, could without further ado refer in a letter written to Plekhanov to 'the famous "hegemony" of Social-Democracy' and call for a political newspaper as the sole effective means of preparing a 'real hegemony' of the working class in Russia.[21] In the event, the emphasis pioneered by Plekhanov and Axelrod on the vocation

---

17  Axelrod, *Istoricheskoe Polozhenie i Vzaimnoe Otnoshenie Liberalnoi i Sotsialisticheskoi Demokratii v Rossii*, Geneva 1898, p. 25.
18  Axelrod, *K Voprosu*, p. 27.
19  *Perepiska G.V. Plekhanova i P.B. Akselroda*, Moscow 1925, II, p. 142.
20  Y. Martov, 'Vsegda v Menshinstve. O Sovremennykh Zadachakh Russkoi Sotsialisticheskoi Intelligentsii', *Zarya*, Nos. 2–3, December 1901, p. 190.
21  Lenin, *Collected Works*, Vol. 34, p. 56.

of the working class to adopt an 'all-national' approach to politics and to fight for the liberation of every oppressed class and group in society was to be developed, with a wholly new scope and eloquence, by Lenin in *What Is to Be Done?* in 1902—a text read and approved in advance by Plekhanov, Axelrod and Potresov, which ended precisely with an urgent plea for the formation of the revolutionary newspaper that was to be *Iskra*.

The slogan of the hegemony of the proletariat in the bourgeois revolution was thus a common political inheritance for Bolsheviks and Mensheviks alike at the Second Congress of the RSDLP in 1903. After the scission, Potresov wrote a lengthy article in *Iskra* reproaching Lenin for his 'primitive' interpretation of the idea of hegemony, summarised in the celebrated call in *What Is to Be Done?* for social-democrats to 'go among all classes of the population' and organise 'special auxiliary detachments' for the working class from them.[22] Potresov complained that the gamut of social classes aimed at by Lenin was too wide, while at the same time the type of relationship he projected between the latter and the proletariat was too peremptory— involving an impossible 'assimilation' rather than an alliance with them. A correct strategy to win hegemony for the working class would betoken an external orientation, not towards such improbable elements as dissident gentry or students, but to democratic liberals, and not denial but respect for their organisational autonomy. Lenin, for his part, was soon accusing the Mensheviks of abandoning the concept by their tacit acceptance of the leadership of Russian capital in the bourgeois revolution against Tsarism. His call for a 'democratic dictatorship of the proletariat and peasantry' in the 1905 revolution was precisely

---

22 A. Potresov, 'Nashi Zakliucheniya. O Liberalizme i Gegemonii', *Iskra*, No. 74, 20 November 1904.

designed to give a governmental formula to the traditional strategy, to which he remained faithful.

After the defeat of the revolution, Lenin vehemently denounced the Mensheviks for their relinquishment of the axiom of hegemony, in a series of major articles in which he again and again reasserted its political indispensability for any revolutionary Marxist in Russia. 'Because the bourgeois-democratic tasks have been left unfulfilled, a revolutionary crisis is still inevitable', he wrote. 'The tasks of the proletariat that arise from this situation are fully and unmistakably definite. As the only consistently revolutionary class of contemporary society, it must be the leader in the struggle of the whole people for a fully democratic revolution, in the struggle of all the working and exploited people against the oppressors and exploiters. The proletariat is revolutionary only in so far as it is conscious of and gives effect to this idea of the hegemony of the proletariat.'[23] Menshevik writers, claiming that since 1905 Tsarism had effected a transition from a feudal to a capitalist state, had recently declared the hegemony of the proletariat to be obsolete, since the bourgeois revolution was now over in Russia.[24] Lenin's response was thunderous: 'To preach to the workers that what they need is "not hegemony, but a class party" means to betray the cause of the proletariat to the liberals; it means preaching that Social-Democratic labour policy should be replaced by a liberal labour policy. Renunciation of the idea of hegemony is the crudest form of reformism in the Russian Social-Democratic movement.'[25]

It was in these polemics, too, that Lenin repeatedly contrasted

---

23 Lenin, *Collected Works*, Vol. 17, pp. 231–2.
24 I have elsewhere discussed the importance of these polemics of 1911, for an account of the nature of Tsarism, in *Lineages of the Absolutist State*, London 1975, pp. 354–5.
25 Lenin, *Collected Works*, Vol. 17, pp. 232–3. See also pp. 78–9.

a 'hegemonic' with a 'guild' or 'corporatist' phase within proletarian politics. 'From the standpoint of Marxism the class, so long as it renounces the idea of hegemony or fails to appreciate it, is not a class, or not yet a class, but a guild, or the sum total of various guilds … It is the consciousness of the idea of hegemony and its implementation through their own activities that converts the guilds (*tsekhi*) as a whole into a class.'[26]

The term hegemony, then, was one of the most widely used and familiar notions in the debates of the Russian labour movement before the October Revolution. After the revolution, it fell into relative disuse in the Bolshevik Party—for one very good reason. Forged to theorise the role of the working class in a bourgeois revolution, it was rendered inoperative by the advent of a socialist revolution. The scenario of a 'democratic dictatorship of workers and peasants' remaining within the bounds of capitalism never materialised, as is well known. Trotsky, who had never believed in the coherence or feasibility of Lenin's programme for 1905, and whose contrary prediction of a socialist revolution had been rapidly vindicated in 1917, later wrote in his *History of the Russian Revolution*: 'The popular and officially accepted idea of hegemony of the proletariat in the democratic revolution … did not at all signify that the proletariat would use a peasant uprising in order with its support to place upon on the order of the day its own historic task—that is, the direct transition to a socialist society. The hegemony of the proletariat in the democratic revolution was sharply distinguished from the dictatorship of the proletariat, and polemically contrasted against it. The Bolshevik Party had been educated in these ideas ever since 1905.'[27] Trotsky was not to know that a 'polemical contrast'

---

26  Ibid., pp. 57–8.
27  Trotsky, *History of the Russian Revolution*, I, London 1965, pp. 296–7.

between the 'hegemony' and the 'dictatorship' of the proletariat would re-emerge again in an altered context, in another epoch.

At the time, in the aftermath of October, the term hegemony ceased to have much internal actuality in the USSR. It survived, however, in the external documents of the Communist International. At the first two World Congresses of the Third International, the Comintern adopted a series of theses which for the first time internationalised Russian usages of the slogan of hegemony. The proletariat's duty was to exercise hegemony over the other exploited groups that were its class allies in the struggle against capitalism, within its own soviet institutions; there 'its hegemony will permit the progressive elevation of the semi-proletariat and poor peasantry'.[28] If it failed to lead the toiling masses in all arenas of social activity, confining itself to its own particularist economic objectives, it would lapse into corporatism. 'The proletariat becomes a revolutionary class only in so far as it does not restrict itself to the framework of a narrow corporatism and acts in every manifestation and domain of social life as the guide of the whole working and exploited population ... The industrial proletariat cannot absolve its world-historical mission, which is the emancipation of mankind from the yoke of capitalism and of war, if it limits itself to its own particular corporative interests and to efforts to improve its situation—sometimes a very satisfactory one—within bourgeois society'.[29] At the Fourth Congress in 1922, the term hegemony was—for what seems to be the first time—extended to the domination of the bourgeoisie over the proletariat, if the former succeeded in confining the latter to a corporate role by inducing it to accept

28  *Manifestes, thèses et résolutions des quatre premiers congrès mondiaux de l'Internationale Communiste 1919–1923*, Paris 1969 (reprint), p. 20.
29  Ibid., pp. 45, 61.

a division between political and economic struggles in its class practice. 'The bourgeoisie always seeks to separate politics from economics, because it understands very well that if it succeeds in keeping the working class within a corporative framework, no serious danger can threaten its hegemony.'[30]

The transmission of the notion of hegemony to Gramsci, from the Russian to the Italian theatres of the socialist movement, can with reasonable certainty be located in these successive documents of the Comintern. The debates of the pre-war RSDLP had become archival after the October Revolution; although Gramsci spent a year in Moscow in 1922–3 and learnt Russian, it is extremely unlikely that he would have had any direct acquaintance with the texts of Axelrod, Martov, Potresov or Lenin which debated the slogan of hegemony. On the other hand, he naturally had an intimate knowledge of the Comintern resolutions of the time: he was, indeed, a participant at the Fourth World Congress itself. The consequences can be seen in the *Prison Notebooks*: for Gramsci's own treatment of the idea of hegemony descends directly from the definitions of the Third International.

We can now revert to Gramsci's texts themselves. Throughout the *Prison Notebooks*, the term 'hegemony' recurs in a multitude of different contexts. Yet there is no doubt that Gramsci started from certain constant connotations of the concept, which he derived from the Comintern tradition. For in the first instance, the term refers in his writings to the class alliance of the proletariat with other exploited groups, above all the peasantry, in a common struggle against the oppression of capital. Reflecting the experience of NEP, he laid a somewhat greater emphasis on the need for 'concessions' and 'sacrifices' by the proletariat to its allies for it to win hegemony over them, thereby extending

---

30  Ibid., p. 171.

the notion of 'corporatism' from a mere confinement to guild horizons or economic struggles to any kind of ouvrierist isolation from the other exploited masses. 'The fact of hegemony presupposes that account is taken of the interests and tendencies of the groups over which hegemony is to be exercised, and that a certain balance of compromise should be formed—in other words that the leading group should make sacrifices of an economico-corporative kind. But there is no doubt that although hegemony is ethico-political, it must also be economic, must necessarily be based on the decisive function exercised by the leading group in the decisive nucleus of economic activity.'[31] At the same time, Gramsci also stressed more eloquently than any Russian Marxist before 1917 the cultural ascendancy which the hegemony of the proletariat over allied classes must involve. 'Previously germinated ideologies become "party", come into conflict and confrontation, until only one of them, or at least a single combination, tends to prevail, gaining the upper hand and propagating itself throughout society. It thereby achieves not only a unison of economic and political aims, but also intellectual and moral unity, posing all questions over which the struggle rages not on a corporate but on a universal plane. It thus creates the hegemony of a fundamental social group over a series of subordinate groups.'[32]

In a further development in the same theoretical direction, Gramsci went on to counterpose the proletariat's necessary use of violence against the common enemy of the exploited classes, and the resort to compromise within these classes. In doing so, he was in effect restating the traditional opposition between 'dictatorship of the proletariat' (over the bourgeoisie) and

31  *QC* III, p. 1591; *SPN*, p. 161.
32  *QC* III, p. 1584; *SPN*, pp. 181–2.

'hegemony of the proletariat' (over the peasantry), so sharply recalled by Trotsky. 'If the union of two forces is necessary in order to defeat a third, a recourse to arms and coercion (even supposing that these are available) can be nothing more than a methodological hypothesis. The only concrete possibility is compromise. Force can be employed against enemies, but not against a part of one's own side which one wants to assimilate rapidly, and whose "goodwill" and enthusiasm one needs.'[33] The 'union' of which Gramsci speaks here acquires a much more pronounced inflection in his texts than in the Bolshevik vocabulary: the mechanical Russian image of the *smychka*—or 'yoking'—of working class and peasantry, popularised during NEP, becomes the organic fusion of a 'new historical bloc' in the *Notebooks*. Thus in the same passage, Gramsci refers to the necessity to 'absorb' allied social forces, in order 'to create a new, homogeneous, politico-economic historical bloc, without internal contradictions'.[34] The heightened register of the formula corresponds to the novel charge given to cultural and moral radiation in Gramsci's usage of hegemony.

So far, the recurrent appeal in the *Prison Notebooks* to the term hegemony represents no major departure from the Russian revolutionary canon from which it was taken. However, the very form of the prison writings was insensibly to shift the signifi- cance and function of the concept, in their context as a whole. For the characteristic medium in which Gramsci presented his ideas was that of a protocol of general axioms of political soci- ology, with 'floating' referents—sometimes allusively specified

---

33  *QC* III, pp. 1612–13; *SPN*, p. 168.
34  *QC* III, p. 1612; *SPN*, p. 168. It will be remembered that Potresov specifically denounced any interpretation of hegemony that involved an 'assimilation' of allied classes.

by class or regime or epoch, but equally often ambiguously evocative of several possible exemplars. This procedure, foreign to any other Marxist, was of course dictated to Gramsci by the need to lull the vigilance of the censor. Its result, however, was a constant indeterminacy of focus, in which the bourgeoisie and the proletariat can often alternate simultaneously as the hypothetical subjects of the same passage—whenever, in fact, Gramsci writes in the abstract of a 'dominant class'. The mask of generalisation into which Gramsci was thus frequently driven had serious consequences for his thought: for it induced the unexamined premise that the structural positions of the bourgeoisie and the proletariat, in their respective revolutions and their successive states, were historically equivalent. The risks of such a tacit comparison will be seen in due course. At present, what is important is to note the way in which the 'desituated' mode of discourse peculiar to so many of the texts of Gramsci's imprisonment permitted an imperceptible transition to a much wider theory of hegemony than had ever been imagined in Russia, which produced a wholly new theoretical field of Marxist enquiry in Gramsci's work.

For in effect, Gramsci extended the notion of hegemony from its original application to the perspectives of the working class in a bourgeois revolution against a feudal order, to the mechanisms of bourgeois rule over the working class in a stabilised capitalist society. There was a precedent for this in the Comintern theses, it will be recollected. Yet the passage in question was brief and isolated: it did not issue into any more developed account of the sway of capital. Gramsci, by contrast, now employed the concept of hegemony for a differential analysis of the structures of bourgeois power in the West. This was a new and decisive step. The passage from one usage to the other was mediated through a set of generic maxims in principle applicable to either. The result was an apparently formal sequence of propositions about the nature of power in history.

Symbolically, Gramsci took Machiavelli's work as his starting-point for this new range of theory. Arguing the necessity of a 'dual perspective' in all political action, he wrote that at their 'fundamental levels', the two perspectives corresponded to the 'dual nature of Machiavelli's Centaur—half-animal and half-human'. For Gramsci, these were 'the levels of force and consent, domination and hegemony, violence and civilisation'.[35] The terrain of discourse here is manifestly universal, in emulation of the manner of Machiavelli himself. An explicit set of oppositions is presented, valid for any historical epoch:

| | |
|---|---|
| Force | Consent |
| Domination | Hegemony |
| Violence | Civilisation |

The term 'domination' which is the antithesis of 'hegemony' recurs in another couplet to be found in other texts, in opposition to 'direction'. In the most important of these, Gramsci wrote: 'The supremacy of a social group assumes two forms: "domination" and "intellectual and moral direction". A social group is dominant over enemy groups which it tends to "liquidate" or subject with armed force, and is directive over affinal and allied groups.'[36] Here, the classical Russian distinction between 'dictatorship' and 'hegemony' is particularly clearly restated, in a slightly new terminology. The critical significance of the passage, however, is that it refers unambiguously not to the proletariat, but to the bourgeoisie—for its subject is the role of the Moderates in the

---

35   QC III, p. 1576; SPN, pp. 169–70.
36   QC III, p. 2010; SPN, p. 57.

Italian Risorgimento, and their ascendancy over the Action Party. In other words, Gramsci has swung the compass of the concept of hegemony towards a study of capitalist rule, albeit still within the context of a bourgeois revolution (the original framework for the notion in Russia). The elision of 'direction' with 'hegemony' is made later in the same paragraph on the Risorgimento.[37] The two are equated straightforwardly in a contemporary letter written by Gramsci, when he remarks that 'Croce emphasises solely that moment in historico-political activity which in politics is called "hegemony", the moment of consent, of cultural direction, to distinguish it from the moment of force, of constraint, of state-legislative or police intervention.'[38]

At the same time, the powerful cultural emphasis that the idea of hegemony acquired in Gramsci's work combined with his theoretical application of it to traditional ruling classes, to produce a new Marxist theory of intellectuals. For one of the classical functions of the latter, Gramsci argued, was to mediate the hegemony of the exploiting classes over the exploited classes via the ideological systems of which they were the organizing agents. Croce himself represented for Gramsci one of those 'great intellectuals who exercise a hegemony that presupposes a certain collaboration, or voluntary and active consent' from the subordinate classes.[39]

The next question that Gramsci posed was specific to his thought. Where are the two functions of 'domination' and 'direction/hegemony' exercised? In particular, what is the site of 'hegemony'? Gramsci's first and firmest answer is that hegemony (direction) pertains to civil society, and coercion (domination) to

---

37   *QC* III, p. 2011; *SPN*, p. 58.
38   *Lettere dal Carcere*, p. 616.
39   *QC* II, p. 691; *SPN*, p. 271.

the state. 'We can now fix two major superstructural levels—one that may be called "civil society", that is the ensemble of organisms commonly called "private", and the other that of "political society" or the state. These two levels correspond on the one hand to the function of "hegemony" which the dominant group exercises throughout society and on the other hand to that of "direct domination" or command exercised through the State and "juridical" government.'[40] There was no precedent for such a theorisation in the Russian debates. The reason is evident. Gramsci was by now unmistakably more concerned with the constellation of bourgeois political power in an orthodox capitalist social order. The allusion to the 'private' institutions of civil society—inappropriate to any social formation in which the working class exercises collective power—indicates the real object of his thought here. In a contemporary letter, Gramsci referred even more directly to the contrast within the context of capitalism, writing of the opposition between political society and civil society as the respective sites of two modes of class power: 'political society (or dictatorship, or coercive apparatus to ensure that the popular masses conform to the type of production and economy of a given moment)' was counterposed to 'civil society (or hegemony of a social group over the whole national society exercised through so-called private organisations, like the church, trade unions, schools and so on)'.[41] Here the listing of church and schools as instruments of hegemony within the private associations of civil society puts the application of the concept to the capitalist societies of the West beyond any doubt. The result is to yield these unambiguous oppositions:

---

40  QC III, pp. 1518–19; SPN, p. 12. The context is precisely a discussion of intellectuals.
41  Lettere del Carcere, p. 481.

| Hegemony | Domination |
|----------|------------|
| = | = |
| Consent | Coercion |
| = | = |
| Civil Society | State |

It has, however, already been seen that Gramsci did not use the antonyms of state and civil society univocally. Both the terms and the relationship between them undergo different mutations in his writings. Exactly the same is true of the term 'hegemony'. For the texts quoted above contrast with others in which Gramsci speaks of hegemony not as a pole of 'consent' in contrast to another of 'coercion', but as itself a synthesis of consent and coercion. Thus, in a note on French political history, he commented: 'The normal exercise of hegemony on the now classical terrain of a parliamentary regime is characterised by a combination of force and consent which form variable equilibria, without force ever prevailing too much over consent.'[42] Here Gramsci's reorientation of the concept of hegemony towards the advanced capitalist countries of Western Europe and the structures of bourgeois power within them acquires a further thematic accentuation. The notion is now directly connected with the phenomenon of parliamentary democracy, peculiar to the West. At the same time, parallel with the shift in the function of hegemony from consent to consent-coercion, there occurs a relocation of its topographical position. For in another passage, Gramsci writes of the executive, legislature and judiciary of the liberal state as 'organs of political hegemony'.[43] Here hegemony is firmly situated within the state—no longer confined to civil society. The

---

42   *QC* III, p. 1638; *SPN*, p. 80n.
43   *QC* II, p. 752; *SPN*, p. 246.

nuance of 'political hegemony', contrasting with 'civil hegemony', underlines the residual opposition between political society and civil society, which as we know is one of Gramsci's variants of the couplet state and civil society. In other words, hegemony is here located not in one of the two terms, but in both.

| State | Civil Society |
|-------|---------------|
| = | = |
| Political Hegemony | Civil Hegemony |

This version cannot be reconciled with the preceding account, which remains the predominant one in the *Notebooks*. For in the first, Gramsci counterposes hegemony to political society or the state, while in the second the state itself becomes an apparatus of hegemony. In yet another version, the distinction between civil and political society disappears altogether: consent and coercion alike become co-extensive with the state. Gramsci writes: 'The State (in its integral meaning) is dictatorship + hegemony.'[44] The oscillations in the connotation and location of hegemony amplify those of the original pair of terms themselves. Thus in the enigmatic mosaic that Gramsci assembled in prison, the words 'state', 'civil society', 'political society', 'hegemony', 'domination' or 'direction' all undergo a persistent slippage. We will now try to show that this slippage is neither accidental nor arbitrary.

---

44   *QC* II, pp. 810–11; *SPN*, p. 239.

# 2

# VARIANTS

Three distinct versions of the relations between Gramsci's key concepts are simultaneously discernible in his *Prison Notebooks*, once the problematic of hegemony shifted away from the social alliances of the proletariat in the East towards the structures of bourgeois power in the West. It will be seen that each of these corresponds to a fundamental problem for Marxist analysis of the bourgeois state, without providing an adequate answer to it: the variation between the versions is precisely the decipherable symptom of Gramsci's awareness of the aporia of his solutions. To indicate the limits of Gramsci's axioms, of course, more than a philological demonstration of their lack of internal coherence is needed. However summary, certain political assessments of their external correspondence with the nature of the contemporary bourgeois states in the West will be suggested.

At the same time, however, these will remain within the limits of Gramsci's own system of categories. The question of whether the latter in fact provide the best point of departure for a scientific analysis of the structures of capitalist power today will not be prejudged. In particular, the binary oppositions of 'state and civil society' and 'coercion and consent' will be respected as the central elements of Gramsci's discourse; it is their application, rather than their function, in his Marxism that will be reviewed. The difficulties of any too-dualist theory of bourgeois class power will not be explored here. It is evident, in effect, that the whole range of directly economic constraints to which the exploited classes within capitalism are subjected cannot immediately be classified within either of the political categories of coercion or consent—armed force or cultural persuasion. Similarly, a formal dichotomy of state and civil society, however necessary as a preliminary instrument, cannot in itself yield specific knowledge of the complex relations between the different institutions of a capitalist social formation (some of which typically occupy intermediate positions on the borders of the two). It is possible that the analytic issues with which Gramsci was most concerned in fact need to be reconceptualised within a new order of categories, beyond his binary landmarks. These problems, however, fall outside the scope of a textual commentary. For our purposes here, it will be sufficient to stay on the terrain of Gramsci's own enquiry—still today that of a pioneer.

We may start by examining the first and most striking configuration of Gramsci's terms cited above, the most important for the ulterior destiny of his work. Its central text is the initial passage cited in this essay, in which Gramsci writes of the difference between East and West, and says that in the East, the 'State is everything', while in the West, the state is an 'outer ditch' of the inner fortress of civil society, which can survive the worst tremors in the state, because it is not 'primordial and gelatinous' as in the East, but robust and structured. A 'war of manoeuvre' is thus appropriate in the East, a 'war of position' in the West. This thesis can then be linked to the companion argument, reiterated in so many other texts, that the state is the site of the armed domination or coercion of the bourgeoisie over the exploited classes, while civil society is the arena of its cultural direction or consensual hegemony over them—the opposition between 'force and consent, coercion and persuasion, state and church, political society and civil society'.[1] The result is to aggregate a combined set of oppositions for the distinction East/West:

| East | West |
|---|---|
| State | Civil Society |
| / | / |
| Civil Society | State |
| Coercion | Consent |
| Domination | Hegemony |
| Manoeuvre | Position |

In other words, the preponderance of civil society over the state in the West can be equated with the predominance of 'hegemony' over 'coercion' as the fundamental mode of bourgeois power in advanced capitalism. Since hegemony pertains to civil society, and civil society prevails over the state, it is the cultural ascendancy of the ruling class that essentially ensures the stability of the capitalist order. For in Gramsci's usage here, hegemony means the ideological subordination of the working class by the bourgeoisie, which enables it to rule by consent.

Now the preliminary aim of this formula is evident. It is to establish one obvious and fundamental difference between Tsarist Russia and Western Europe—the existence of representative political democracy. As such, it is analogous to Lenin's lapidary formula that the Russian Tsars ruled by force and the Anglo-French bourgeoisie by deception and concessions.[2] The

---

1    *QC* II, p. 763; *SPN*, p. 170.
2    'The worldwide experience of bourgeois and landowner governments has evolved two methods of keeping people in subjection. The first is violence,'

great theoretical merit of Gramsci was to have posed the problem of this difference far more persistently and coherently than any other revolutionary before or since. Nowhere in the writings of Lenin or Trotsky, or other Bolshevik theorists, can there be found any sustained or systematic reflection on the enormous historical divide within Europe traced by the presence—even if still fitful and incomplete in their time—of parliamentary democracy in the West, and its absence in the East. A problem registered at most in marginal asides in the Bolshevik tradition was developed for the first time into a commanding theme for Marxist theory by Gramsci.

At the same time, the first solution he sketches in the *Prison Notebooks* is radically unviable: the simple location of 'hegemony' within civil society, and the attribution of primacy to civil society over the state. This equation, in effect, corresponds very exactly to what might be called a common-sense view of bourgeois democracy in the West on the left—a view widely diffused in militant social-democratic circles since the Second World War.[3] For this conception, the State in the West is not a violent machine of police repression as it was in Tsarist Russia: the masses have access to it through regular democratic elections, which formally permit the possibility of a socialist government. Yet experience shows that these elections never produce a government dedicated to the expropriation of capital

---

with which the Tsars 'demonstrated to the Russian people the maximum of what can and cannot be done', Lenin wrote. 'But there is another method, best developed by the British and French bourgeoisie ... the method of deception, flattery, fine phrases, promises by the million, petty sops, and concessions of the unessential while retaining the essential.' *Collected Works*, Vol. 24, pp. 63–4.

3   The first major interpretation of Gramsci of this sort was the work of a PSI theorist: Giuseppe Tamburrano, *Antonio Gramsci. La vita, il pensiero, l'azione*, Bari 1963.

and the realisation of socialism. Fifty years after the advent of universal suffrage, such a phenomenon seems further away than ever. What is the reason for this paradox? It must lie in the prior ideological conditioning of the proletariat before the electoral moment as such. The central locus of power must therefore be sought within civil society—above all, in capitalist control of the means of communication (press, radio, television, cinema, publishing), based on control of the means of production (private property). In a more sophisticated variant, the real inculcation of voluntary acceptance of capitalism occurs not so much through the ideological indoctrination of the means of communication, as in the invisible diffusion of commodity fetishism through the market or the instinctual habits of submission induced by the work-routines of factories and offices—in other words, directly within the ambit of the means of production themselves. Yet whether the primary emphasis is given to the effect of cultural or economic apparatuses, the analytic conclusion is the same. It is the strategic nexus of civil society which is believed to maintain capitalist hegemony within a political democracy, whose state institutions do not directly debar or repress the masses.[4] The system is maintained by consent, not coercion. Therefore the main task of socialist militants is not combat with an armed state, but ideological conversion of the working class to free it from submission to capitalist mystifications.

This characteristic syndrome of left social democracy contains a number of illusions. The first and most immediate of its errors is precisely the notion that the ideological power of the bourgeoisie in Western social formations is exercised above all in

---

4   For a representative version of these ideas, see Perry Anderson, 'Problems of Socialist Strategy', in the collection *Towards Socialism*, London 1965, pp. 223–47.

the sphere of civil society, its hegemony over which subsequently neutralises the democratic potential of the representative state. The working class has access to the state (elections to parliament), but does not exercise it to achieve socialism because of its indoctrination by the means of communication. In fact, it might be said that the truth is if anything the inverse: the general form of the representative state—bourgeois democracy —is itself the principal ideological linchpin of Western capitalism, whose very existence deprives the working class of the idea of socialism as a different type of state, and the means of communication and other mechanisms of cultural control thereafter clinch this central ideological 'effect'. Capitalist relations of production allocate all men and women into different social classes, defined by their differential access to the means of production. These class divisions are the underlying reality of the wage-contract between juridically free and equal persons that is the hallmark of this mode of production. The political and economic orders are thereby formally separated under capitalism. The bourgeois state thus by definition 'represents' the totality of the population, abstracted from its distribution into social classes, as individual and equal citizens. In other words, it presents to men and women their unequal positions in civil society as if they were equal in the state. Parliament, elected every four or five years as the sovereign expression of popular will, reflects the fictive unity of the nation back to the masses as if it were their own self-government. The economic divisions within the 'citizenry' are masked by the juridical parity between exploiters and exploited, and with them the complete separation and non-participation of the masses in the work of parliament. This separation is then constantly presented and represented to the masses as the ultimate incarnation of liberty: 'democracy' as the terminal point of history. The existence of the parliamentary state thus constitutes the formal framework of all other ideological mechanisms of the ruling class. It provides the general code in which every specific message elsewhere is transmitted. The code is all the more powerful because the juridical rights of citizenship are not a mere mirage: on the contrary, the civic freedoms and suffrages of bourgeois democracy are a tangible reality, whose completion was historically in part the work of the labour movement itself, and whose loss would be a momentous defeat for the working class.[5]

By comparison, the economic improvements won by reforms within the framework of the representative state—apparently more material—have typically left less ideological mark on the masses in the West. In the leading imperialist countries, the steady rise in the standard of living of the working class for twenty-five years after the Second World War has been a critical element in the political stability of metropolitan capitalism. Yet the material component of popular assent to it, the subject of traditional polemics over the effects of reformism, is inherently unstable and volatile, since it tends to create a constant progression of expectations whose satisfaction no national capitalist economy can totally ensure, even during long waves of international boom, let alone phases of recession; its very 'dynamism' is thus potentially destabilizing and capable of provoking crises

---

5    In other words, it is quite wrong simply to designate parliament an 'ideological apparatus' of bourgeois power without further ado. The ideological function of parliamentary sovereignty is inscribed in the formal framework of every bourgeois constitution, and is always central to the cultural dominion of capital. However, parliament is also, of course, a 'political apparatus', vested with real attributes of debate and decision, which are in no sense a mere subjective trick to lull the masses. They are objective structures of a once-great—still potent—historical achievement, the triumph of the ideals of the bourgeois revolution.

when growth fluctuates or stalls. By contrast, the juridico-political component of consent induced by the parliamentary state is much more stable: the capitalist polity is not subject to the same conjunctural vicissitudes. The historical occasions on which it has been actively questioned by working class struggles have been infinitely fewer in the West. In other words, the ideology of bourgeois democracy is far more potent than that of any welfare reformism, and forms the permanent syntax of the consensus instilled by the capitalist state.

It can now be seen why Gramsci's primary formula was mistaken. It is impossible to partition the ideological functions of bourgeois class power between civil society and the state, in the way that he initially sought to do. The fundamental form of the Western parliamentary state—the juridical sum of its citizenry—is itself the hub of the ideological apparatuses of capitalism. The ramified complexes of the cultural control systems within civil society—radio, television, cinema, churches, newspapers, political parties—undoubtedly play a critical complementary role in assuring the stability of the class order of capital. So too, of course, do the distorting prism of market relations and the numbing structure of the labour process within the economy. The importance of these systems should certainly not be underestimated. But neither should it be exaggerated or—above all—counterposed to the cultural-ideological role of the state itself.

A certain vulgar leftism has traditionally isolated the problem of consent from its structural context, and hypostasised it as the unique and distinguishing feature of capitalist rule in the West, which becomes reduced to the sobriquet of 'parliamentarism'. To refute this error, many Marxists have pointed out that all ruling classes in history have normally obtained the consent of the exploited classes to their own exploitation—feudal lords or slave-owning latifundists no less than industrial entrepreneurs. The objection is, of course, correct. But it is not an adequate reply, unless it is accompanied by an accurate definition of the *differentia specifica* of the consent won from the working class to the accumulation of capital in the West today—in other words the form and content of the bourgeois ideology which it is induced to accept. Nicos Poulantzas, whose work *Political Power and Social Classes* contains many critically acute comments on the *Prison Notebooks*, in effect dismisses Gramsci's concern with the problem, remarking that the only novelty of this consent is its claim to rationality—i.e. its non-religious character. 'The specific characteristic of (capitalist) ideologies is not at all, as Gramsci believed, that they procure a more or less active "consent" from the dominated classes towards political domination, since this is a general characteristic of any dominant ideology. What specifically defines the ideologies in question is that they do not aim to be accepted by the dominated classes according to the principle of participation in the sacred: they explicitly declare themselves and are accepted as scientific techniques.'[6] In a similar fashion, Ernest Mandel has written in his *Late Capitalism* that the major contemporary form of capitalist ideology in the West is an appeal to technological rationality and a cult of experts: 'Belief in the omnipotence of technology is the specific form of bourgeois ideology in late capitalism.'[7] These claims involve a serious misconception.

For the peculiarity of the historical consent won from the masses within modern capitalist social formations is by no

6  Nicos Poulantzas, *Political Power and Social Classes*, London 1973, p. 217.
7  Ernest Mandel, *Late Capitalism*, London 1975, p. 501.

means to be found in its mere secular reference or technical awe. The novelty of this consent is that it takes the fundamental form of a belief by the masses that they exercise an ultimate self-determination within the existing social order. It is thus not acceptance of the superiority of an acknowledged ruling class (feudal ideology), but credence in the democratic equality of all citizens in the government of the nation—in other words, disbelief in the existence of any ruling class. The consent of the exploited in a capitalist social formation is thus of a qualitatively new type, which has suggestively produced its own etymological extension: consensus, or mutual agreement. Naturally, the active pressure of bourgeois ideology coexists and combines in a wide number of mixed forms with much older and less articulated ideological habits and traditions—in particular, those of passive resignation to the way of the world and diffidence in any possibility of changing it, generated by the differential knowledge and confidence characteristic of any class society.[8] The legacy of these diuturnal traditions does indeed often take the modern guise of deference to technical necessity. They do not, however, represent any real departure from previous patterns of class domination; the condition of their continued efficacy today is their insertion into an ideology of representative democracy which overarches them. For it is the freedom of bourgeois democracy alone that appears to establish the limits of what is socially possible for the collective will of a people, and thereby can render the bounds of its impotence tolerable.[9]

---

8   See the stimulating comments in Göran Therborn, 'What does the Ruling Class do when it Rules?', *The Insurgent Sociologist*, Vol. VI, No. 3, Spring 1976.

9   A real and central belief in popular sovereignty can, in other words, coexist with a profound scepticism towards all governments that juridically express it. The divorce between the two is typically mediated by the conviction that

Variants ✳ 69

Gramsci himself was, in fact, very conscious of the need
for careful discrimination of the successive historical forms of
'consent' by the exploited to their exploitation, and for analytic
differentiation of its components at any one moment of time. He
reproached Croce precisely for assuming in his *History of Liberty*
that all ideologies prior to liberalism were of the 'same sere and
indistinct colour, devoid of development or conflict'—stressing
the specificity of the hold of religion on the masses of Bourbon
Naples, the power of the appeal to the nation which succeeded
it in Italy, and at the same time the possibility of popular combinations of the two.[10] Elsewhere, he contrasted the epochs of the
French Revolution and Restoration in Europe precisely in terms
of the distinct types of consent—'direct' and 'indirect'—that they
obtained from the oppressed, and the forms of suffrage—universal and censitary—that corresponded to them.[11] Paradoxically,
however, Gramsci never produced any comprehensive account
of the history or structure of bourgeois democracy in his *Prison
Notebooks*. The problem that confers its deepest meaning on his
central theoretical work remains the horizon rather than the
object of his texts. Part of the reason why the initial equations of
his discourse on hegemony were miscalculated, was due to this
absence. Gramsci was not wrong in his constant reversion to the

---

no government could be otherwise than distant from those it represents,
yet many are not representative at all. This is not a mere fatalism or cyni-
cism among the masses in the West. It is an active assent to the familiar
order of bourgeois democracy, as the dull maximum of liberty, that is
constantly reproduced by the radical absence of proletarian democracy in
the East, whose regimes figure the infernal minimum. There is no
space to explore the effects of fifty years of Stalinism here: their importance is
enormous for understanding the complex historical meaning of bourgeois
democracy in the West today.

10  *QC* II, pp. 1236–7.
11  *QC* I, p. 443.

problem of consent in the West: until the full nature and role of bourgeois democracy is grasped, nothing can be understood of capitalist power in the advanced industrial countries today. At the same time, it should be clear why Gramsci was mistaken in his first location of 'consent' within civil society. For, in fact, the very nature of this consent excludes such an allocation, since it is precisely the parliamentary representative state that first and foremost induces it.

Let us now look at Gramsci's second version of the relationship between his terms. In this, he no longer ascribes to civil society a preponderance over the state, or a unilateral localisation of hegemony to civil society. On the contrary, civil society is presented as in balance or equilibrium with the state, and hegemony is distributed between state—or 'political society'— and civil society, while itself being redefined to combine coercion and consent. These formulations express Gramsci's unease with his first version, and his acute awareness—despite and against it—of the central ideological role of the Western capitalist state. He does not merely register this role in general. Yet his comments on the particular dimensions of the state which specialise in the performance of it are selective, focusing on its subordinate rather than its superordinate institutions. For Gramsci's specific references to the ideological functions of the state are concerned not so much with parliament, as with education and law—the school system and the judicial system. 'Every State is ethical in so far as one of its most important functions is to elevate the great mass of the population to a given cultural and moral level, a level or standard which corresponds to the needs of development of the forces of production and hence to the interests of the dominant classes. The school as a positive educational function and the courts as a negative and repressive educational function are the most important such activities of the State. But in reality a multiplicity of other so-called private initiatives and activities tend towards the same end, which constitute the apparatus of political and cultural hegemony of the ruling class.'[12]

This emphasis is extremely important. It underlines all the distance between Gramsci and many of his later commentators, whatever the limits of Gramsci's development of it. Yet at the same time, it cannot be accepted as a true correction of the first version. Gramsci now grasps the co-presence of ideological controls within civil society and the state. But this gain on one plane is offset by a loss of clarity on another. Hegemony, which was earlier allocated to civil society only, is now exercised by the state as well. Simultaneously, however, its meaning tends to change: it now no longer indicates cultural supremacy alone, for it also includes coercion. 'The normal exercise of hegemony' is now 'characterised by a combination of force and consent'. The result is that Gramsci now commits an error from the other direction. For coercion is precisely a legal monopoly of the capitalist state. In Weber's famous definition, the state is the institution which enjoys a monopoly of legitimate violence over a given territory.[13] It alone possesses an army and a police—'groups of men specialised in the use of repression' (Engels). Thus it is not true that hegemony as coercion + consent is co-present in civil society and the state alike. The exercise of repression is juridically absent from civil society. The state reserves it as an exclusive domain.[14] This brings us to a first fundamental axiom governing

---

12 *QC* II, p. 1049. See also *QC* III, p. 1570; *SPN*, p. 246.
13 'Politics as a Vocation', in *From Max Weber*, ed. Gerth and Mills, London 1948, p. 78.
14 This is a regulative principle of any modern capitalist state. It naturally permits of certain variations and qualifications in practice. The state's

the nature of power in a developed capitalist social formation. There is always a structural asymmetry in the distribution of the consensual and coercive functions of this power. Ideology is shared between civil society and the state: violence pertains to the state alone. In other words, the state enters twice over into any equation between the two.

It is possible that one reason why Gramsci had difficulty in isolating this asymmetry was that Italy had witnessed in 1920–2 the exceptional emergence of military squads organised by the fascists, which operated freely outside the state apparatus proper. The structural monopoly of violence by the capitalist state was thus to some extent masked by conjunctural commando operations (Gramsci's term) within civil society. Yet in fact, of course, the *squadristi* could only assault and sack working class institutions with impunity because they had the tacit coverage of the police and army. Gramsci, with his customary lucidity, was naturally well aware of this: 'In the present struggles it often happens that a weakened State machine is like a flagging army: commandos, or private armed organisations, enter the field to accomplish two tasks—to use illegality, while the State appears to remain within legality, and thereby to reorganise the State itself.'[15] Commenting on the March on Rome, he wrote: 'There could be no "civil war" between the State and the fascist movement, only a sporadic violent action to modify the leadership of the State and reform its administrative apparatus. In the civil

---

monopoly of the means of coercion may be legally drawn at the line of automatic weapons, rather than handguns, as in the USA or Switzerland. There may be semi-legal organisations of private violence, such as the American goon-squads of the twenties and thirties. Gramsci was certainly impressed by the existence of the latter. However, these phenomena have always been of marginal importance compared with the central machinery of the state, in the advanced capitalist social formations.

15   *QC* I, p. 121; *SPN*, p. 232.

guerrilla struggle, the fascist movement was not against the State, but aligned with it.'[16] The relatively atypical episode of the fascist squads—whose expeditions could only be 'sporadic'—does not in fact seem to have had any notable effect on the balance of Gramsci's thought.

More important for the uncertainty of his account of the relationship between state and civil society in this respect was the recurrent tendency of his theory towards an over-extension of its concepts. His dissolution of the police into a wider and vaguer social phenomenon is a not untypical example. 'What is the police? It is certainly not merely the official organisation, juridically acknowledged and assigned to the function of public security, that is usually understood by the term. The latter is the central nucleus that has formal responsibility for the "police", which is actually a much vaster organisation, in which a large part of the population of a State participates, directly or indirectly, with more or less precise and definite links, permanently or occasionally.'[17] In fact, it is striking that in precisely the area of law, which particularly interested him as a function of the state, Gramsci could simultaneously note the absence of any coercive equivalent to its sanctions within civil society, yet argue that legality should nevertheless be regarded as a more ubiquitous system of pressures and compulsions at work in civil society as much as in the state, to produce particular moral and cultural standards. 'The concept of "law" should be extended to include those activities which today are designated "juridically neutral" and are within the domain of civil society, which operates without taxative sanctions or obligations, but nonetheless exercises a collective pressure and obtains objective results in

16   *QC* II, pp. 808–9.
17   *QC* I, pp. 279–80.

determining customs, ways of thinking and behaving, morals, and so on.'[18] The result is a structural indistinction between law and custom, juridical rules and conventional norms, which impedes accurate demarcation of the respective provinces of civil society or the state in a capitalist social formation. Gramsci was never quite able to fix the asymmetry between the two: his successive formulations constantly grope towards it, without ever exactly reaching it.

For Gramsci's third version of relationship between his terms represents a final attempt to grasp his elusive object. In this version, the state now includes 'political society' and 'civil society' alike. In effect, it radicalises the categorial fusion incipient in the second version. There is now no longer merely a distribution of hegemony, as a synthesis of coercion and consent, across state and civil society. State and civil society themselves are merged into a larger suzerain unity. 'By the State should be understood not merely the governmental apparatus, but also the "private" apparatus of hegemony or civil society.'[19] The conclusion of this argument is the abrupt dictum: 'In reality civil society and State are one and the same.'[20] In other words, the state becomes coextensive with the social formation, as in international usage. The concept of civil society as a distinct entity disappears. 'Civil society is also part of the "State", indeed is the State itself.'[21] These formulations can be said to reveal Gramsci's frequent awareness that the role of the state in some sense 'exceeds' that of civil society in the West. They thus constitute an important correction of his second version. Yet once again, the gain on the

---

18   *QC* III, p. 1566; *SPN*, p. 242.
19   *QC* II, p. 801; *SPN*, p. 261.
20   *QC* III, p. 1590; *SPN*, p. 160.
21   *QC* III, p. 2303; *SPN*, p. 261.

new terrain is accompanied by a loss on the previous one. For in this final version, the very distinction between state and civil society is itself cancelled. This solution has grave consequences, which undermine any scientific attempt to define the specificity of bourgeois democracy in the West.

The results can be seen in the adoption of this version by Louis Althusser and his colleagues. For if the first version of Gramsci's equations was above all appropriated by left currents within European social democracy after the war, the third version has been more recently utilised by left currents within European communism. The origins of this adoption can be found in a well-known passage of *For Marx*, in which Althusser, equating the notion of 'civil society' with 'individual economic behaviour' and attributing its descent to Hegel, dismissed it as alien to historical materialism.[22] In fact, of course, while the young Marx did use the term primarily to refer to the sphere of economic needs and activities, it is far from the case that it disappears from his mature writings. If its earlier signification disappears from *Capital* (with the emergence of the concepts of forces/relations of production), the term itself does not—for it had another meaning for Marx, that was not synonymous with individual economic needs, but was a generic designation for all non-state institutions in a capitalist social formation. Marx not only never abandoned this function of the concept of 'civil society', his later political writings repeatedly revolve on a central usage of it. Thus the whole of *The Eighteenth Brumaire* is built on an analysis of Bonapartism which starts from the assertion that: 'The State enmeshes, controls, regulates, supervises and regiments civil society from the most all-embracing expressions of its life down

---

22  *For Marx*, London 1970, p. 110.

to its most insignificant motions, from its most general modes of existence down to the private life of individuals.'[23]

It was this usage which Gramsci took over in his prison writings. In doing so, however, he delimited the concept of 'civil society' much more precisely. In Gramsci, civil society does not refer to the sphere of economic relations, but is precisely contrasted with it as a system of superstructural institutions that is intermediary between economy and state.

'Between the economic structure and the State, with its legislation and coercion, stands civil society.'[24] This is why Gramsci's list of the institutions of hegemony in civil society rarely includes factories or plants—precisely the economic apparatuses that many of his disciples today believe to be primary in inculcating ideological subordination among the masses. (If anything, in his Turin writings, if not in his notes on Americanism in prison, Gramsci often tended to regard the discipline of these as schools of socialism rather than capitalism.) Gramsci's definition of the term 'civil society' can thus be described as a refinement of its

---

23  Marx, *Surveys from Exile*, p. 186. 'The Civil War in France' is the pendant work that provides a theory of the diametric opposite of Bonapartism: 'The direct antithesis to the Empire was the Commune ... The unity of the nation was not to be broken, but, on the contrary, to be organised by the Communal constitution and to become a reality by the destruction of the state power which claimed to be the embodiment of that unity independent of, and superior to, the nation itself ... its legitimate functions were to be wrested from an authority usurping pre-eminence over society itself, and restored to the responsible agents of society.' Marx, *The First International and After*, London 1974, pp. 208, 210. The 'Critique of the Gotha Programme' repeats the same contrast: 'Freedom consists in converting the State from an organ superimposed on society into one thoroughly subordinate to it.' (ibid, p. 354). The term 'civil society' is abbreviated to 'society' in Marx's later work, in all probability because of the ambiguity of the German *bürgerliche Gesellschaft*, but it clearly occupies the same structural position in these contrasts between state and society.

24  *QC* II, p. 1253; *SPN*, p. 208.

use in the late Marx, explicitly dissociating it from its economic origins. At the same time, we have just seen that in his last version of the dyad state and civil society he abandons the distinction between the two altogether, to proclaim their identity. Can the term, however, be simply rejected even in its non-economic usage? There is no question that its variegated passage through Locke, Ferguson, Rousseau, Kant, Hegel and Marx has loaded it with multiple ambiguities and confusions.[25] It will doubtless be necessary to frame a new and unequivocal concept in the future, within a developed theory of the total articulation of capitalist social formations. But until this is available, the term 'civil society' remains a necessary practico-indicative concept, to designate all those institutions and mechanisms outside the boundaries of the state system proper. In other words, its function is to draw an indispensable line of demarcation within the politico-ideological superstructures of capitalism.

Once he had rejected the notion of civil society, Althusser was thus later logically led to a drastic assimilation of Gramsci's final formula, which effectively abolishes the distinction between state and civil society. The result was the thesis that 'churches, parties, trade unions, families, schools, newspapers, cultural ventures' in fact all constitute 'Ideological State Apparatuses'.[26] Explaining this notion, Althusser declared: 'It is unimportant

25 For successive usages of the term, from the Enlightenment onwards, see Bobbio, 'Gramsci e la concezione della società civile', op. cit., pp. 80–4. Prior to Hegel, 'civil society' was customarily opposed to 'natural society' or 'primitive society', as civilisation to nature, rather than to 'political society' or 'state', as divisions within civilisation.

26 *Lenin and Philosophy and other essays*, London 1971, pp. 136–7. Althusser commented: 'To my knowledge, Gramsci is the only one who went any distance down the road I am taking ... Unfortunately, Gramsci did not systematise his intuitions, which remained in the state of acute but fragmentary notes.'

whether the institutions in which they (ideologies) are realised are "public" or "private"'—for these all indifferently form sectors of a single controlling state which is 'the precondition for any distinction between public and private'.[27] The political reasons for this sudden and arbitrary theoretical decision are not entirely clear. However, it seems probable that they were in large measure a product of the attraction exercised by the Chinese Cultural Revolution in the late sixties on semi-oppositional sectors of the European Communist Parties. The revolutionary character officially claimed for the process in China could, in effect, only be squared with classical Marxist definitions of a revolution—the overthrow and destruction of a state machine—by decreeing all manifestations of culture to be state apparatuses.[28] In the Chinese press of the time such manifestations were, indeed, typically discerned in the psychological traits displayed by individuals. To provide Marxist credentials for this 'revolution of the spirits' underway in China, a radical redefinition of the state was necessary. There is little need to dwell today on the inadequacy of this procedure for any rational account of the Cultural Revolution, now an archivised chapter in the history of the CCP. Much more serious were its potential consequences for a responsible socialist politics in the West.

For once the position is adopted that all ideological and political superstructures—including the family, reformist trade

---

27  *Lenin and Philosophy*, pp. 137–8. Once this argument is accepted, of course, there is no reason why not only bourgeois newspapers or families but also capitalist factories and offices should not be dubbed 'State apparatuses'—a conclusion at which Althusser, to his credit, evidently baulked. (Nothing would be easier thereafter than to announce the identity of the 'State bourgeoisie' in the USSR and the bourgeoisie in the USA.) This omission, however, merely serves to suggest the lack of seriousness of the whole trope.

28  See the perceptive remarks in Isaac Deutscher's interview on the Cultural Revolution, *La Sinistra*, Vol. 1, No. 2, November 1966, pp. 13–16.

unions and parties, and private media—are by definition state apparatuses, in strict logic it becomes impossible and unnecessary to distinguish between bourgeois democracies and fascism. For the fact that in the latter total state control over trade unions or mass media was institutionalised would, according to this reasoning, be—to use Althusser's phrase—'unimportant'. A similar conflation of state and civil society could conversely lead younger disciples of the Frankfurt School at the same time to argue that 'liberal democracy' in post-war Germany was functionally equivalent to fascism in pre-war Germany, since the family now fulfilled the authoritarian instance previously occupied by the police, as part of the state system. The unscientific character of such theses is obvious; the European working class paid heavily for anticipations of them in the twenties and early thirties. The boundaries of the state are not a matter of indifference to Marxist theory or revolutionary practice. It is essential to be able to chart them accurately. To blur them is, in fact, to misunderstand the specific role and efficacy of the superstructures outside the state within bourgeois democracy. Ralph Miliband, in a prescient criticism of the whole notion of 'Ideological State Apparatuses', correctly emphasised this. 'To suggest that the relevant institutions are actually part of the State system does not seem to me to accord with reality, and tends to obscure the difference in this respect between these political systems and systems where ideological institutions are indeed part of a State monopolistic system of power. In the former systems, ideological institutions do retain a very high degree of autonomy; and are therefore the better able to conceal the degree to which they do belong to the system of capitalist power.'[29]

---

29 'The Capitalist State: A Reply to Nicos Poulantzas', *New Left Review* 59, January–February 1970, p. 59. Poulantzas, however, can certainly not be

So far as Althusser was concerned, it would in fact have been unjust to ascribe any identification of the structures of fascism and bourgeois democracy to him: there is no sign that he was ever tempted by such ultra-leftist errors—or, alternatively, by the reformist consequences that could also be formally deduced from the idea that trade-union locals or cinema studios were part of the state apparatus in the West (in which case the victory of a communist slate or the making of a militant film would puta-tively count as gradual conquests of 'parts' of a divisible state apparatus—in defiance of the fundamental Marxist tenet of the political unity of the bourgeois state which precisely necessitates a revolution to end it). The reason for the actual innocuousness of a theory that was so potentially dangerous lay in its inspira-tion. Designed for an arcane compliance with events in China,

---

charged with indifference to the problem of the fascist state. His remark-able work, *Fascism and Dictatorship*, London 1974, represents a rare example of theoretical and empirical synthesis in contemporary Marxist literature. While retaining the etiquette of 'Ideological State Apparatuses' in vogue at the time, Poulantzas nevertheless argued that 'this in no way means that the "private" or "public" character of the Ideological State Apparatuses is of no importance', and sought to define the specificity of the fascist state by its reorganisation of the respective branches of the state apparatus into a new and more centralised pattern (pp. 305, 315–30). If his account of the latter remains finally insufficient, it is because his general explanation of the nature of fascism suffers from a certain historical under-determination. Internally, it tends to minimise the acuity of the class threat from the proletariat that evoked it (working class defeat is held to have preceded fascist victory in Italy and Germany—in which case fascism would have been supererogatory for the bourgeoisie), while externally it neglects the dynamics of inter-imperialist struggle (the Second World War is omitted altogether, and with it decisive revelations of the social nature and rationale of fascist expansionism). A more drastic theo-retical delimitation of the fascist states from the bourgeois democracies would follow from any study of these determinants. Given their absence, however, the scope and quality of Poulantzas's work remain all the more impressive.

its exoteric applications in the West lacked any local impetus. The real mark of the thesis was not its political gravity for the working class, so much as its levity.

The case of Gramsci was naturally very different. No distant political determinant was at work in his theorisations of the relationship between state and civil society. The difficulties and contradictions of his texts were rather a reflection of the impediments of his imprisonment. There was, however, a philosophical determinant of his tendency to distend the frontiers of the state. For Gramsci did not produce the idea of an indefinite extension of the state as a political structure from nowhere. He took it, quite directly, from Benedetto Croce. No less than four times in the *Prison Notebooks*, Gramsci cited Croce's view that the 'State' was a higher entity, not to be identified with mere empirical government, that could at times find its real expression in what might seem institutions or arenas of civil society. 'Croce goes so far as to assert that the true "State", that is the directing force in the historical process, is sometimes to be found not where it is usually believed to be, in the State as juridically defined, but often in "private" forces, and sometimes in so-called revolutionaries. This proposition of Croce's is very important for a comprehension of his conception of history and politics.'[30] The metaphysical character of Croce's conception is, of course, manifest: the idea of a numinous essence of the state, floating above mere juridical or institutional appearances, was a typically Hegelian heritage.

---

30 *QC* III, p. 1302. The same idea is cited in *QC* II, p. 858; *QC* II, p. 1087; *QC* II, pp. 1223–4. Gramsci objected to Croce's undue generalisation of his thesis, but he accepted its validity as a principle. 'The claim is not paradoxical for the theory of State-hegemony-moral consciousness, because it can in fact happen that the moral and political direction of a country in a given epoch is not exercised by the legal government, but by a "private" organisation or even a revolutionary party.'

Its reproduction by a strenuously anti-Hegelian school within Western Marxism has a peculiar irony.

This speculative and anti-scientific legacy of Croce's thought undoubtedly had its effects on Gramsci's work. An example of the vagaries for which it was responsible is a text from the *Notebooks* in which Gramsci entertains the idea that parliament might, in certain cases, not be part of the state at all.[31] The misguided direction in which the Crocean fancy led is evident in all those passages of Gramsci's writings which assert or suggest a dissolution of the boundaries between state and civil society. At the same time, however, it is noticeable that wherever Gramsci had to speak directly of the experience of fascism in Italy, he never mistook the significance of the delimitation between the two. For fascism precisely tended to suppress this boundary in practice, and once political concerns proper were primary, Gramsci had no difficulty in registering historical realities. 'With the events of 1924–6, when all political parties were suppressed', he wrote, 'the coincidence of *pays réel* and *pays légal* was henceforward proclaimed in Italy, because civil society in all its forms was now integrated into a single party-political organisation of the State.'[32] Gramsci had no illusions about the significance of the innovations imposed by the counterrevolutionary dictatorship of which he was a victim. 'The contemporary dictatorships juridically abolish even the modern forms of autonomy' of the subordinate classes, he wrote—such as 'parties, trade unions, cultural associations'—and so 'seek to incorporate them into the activity of the State: the legal centralisation of all national life in the hands of a ruling group that is now "totalitarian".'[33]

---

31   *QC* III, pp. 1707–8; *SPN*, pp. 253–4.
32   *QC* III, p. 2058.
33   *QC* III, p. 2287; *SPN*, p. 540.

Thus whatever analytic errors were due to Croce's influence in Gramsci's texts, the aberration of equating fascist and parliamentary forms of the capitalist state was not among them.

The oscillations in Gramsci's usage of his central terms have been noted: he never unambiguously committed himself to any of them. It can, nevertheless, be said that his third version of the relationship between state and civil society—identification—is a reminder that in his prison writings there is no comprehensive comparison of bourgeois democracy and fascism. The problem of the specific difference between the two remains in a sense unresolved in them, which is partly why Gramsci—victim of a police dictatorship in a relatively backward European country—could paradoxically appear after the Second World War as the theorist *par excellence* of the parliamentary state of the advanced capitalist countries. The importance of an operational distinction between state and civil society is posed with particular urgency, as we have seen, for any such comparative analysis. Gramsci's third version in the end tends to suppress the central theoretical problem of his first two versions. The Gordian knot of the relationship between state and civil society in Western social formations, as distinct from Tsarist Russia, is cut by peremptorily decreeing that the state is coextensive with the social formation anyway. The problem, however, remains, and the greater number of Gramsci's texts devoted to exploring his first equations testify to his undiminished consciousness of it.

# 3

# ASYMMETRY

Keeping for the moment to the terms of the *Prison Notebooks*,[1] it has been seen that the key distribution, which eludes each of Gramsci's successive versions, although they miss it from

---

1   The caution should be repeated. The dualist analysis to which Gramsci's notes typically tend does not permit an adequate treatment of economic constraints that act directly to enforce bourgeois class power: among others, the fear of unemployment or dismissal that can, in certain historical circumstances, produce a 'silenced majority' of obedient citizens and pliable voters among the exploited. Such constraints involve neither the conviction of consent, nor the violence of coercion. Their importance has, it is true, diminished with the post-war consolidation of bourgeois democracies in the West, compared with the role of earlier patronage or cacique systems. However, their lesser forms remain myriad in the day-to-day workings of a capitalist society. Another mode of class power that escapes Gramsci's main typology is corruption—consent by purchase, rather than by persuasion, without any ideological fastening. Gramsci was, of course, by no means unaware of either 'constraint' or 'corruption'. He thought, for example, that political liberties in the USA were largely negated by 'economic pressures' (*QC* III, p. 1666); while in France during the Third Republic, he noted that 'between consent and force stood corruption/fraud,' or the neutralisation of movements of opposition by bribery of their leaders, characteristic of conjunctures in which the use of force was too risky (*QC* III, p. 1638; *SPN*, p. 80n). However, he never intercalated them to form a more sophisticated spectrum of concepts systematically into his main theory. The comments below deliberately remain within the confines of the latter.

different directions, is an asymmetry between civil society and the state in the West: coercion is located in the one, consent is located in both. This 'topological' answer, however, itself poses a further and deeper problem. Beyond their distribution, what is the interrelation or connexion between consent and coercion in the structure of bourgeois class power in metropolitan capitalism? The workings of bourgeois democracy appear to justify the idea that advanced capitalism fundamentally rests on the consent of the working class to it. In fact, acceptance of this conception is the cornerstone of the strategy of the 'parliamentary road to socialism', along which progress can be measured by the conversion of the proletariat to the prospect of socialism, until an arithmetical majority is achieved, whereupon the rule of the parliamentary system makes the enactment of socialism painlessly possible. The idea that the power of capital essentially or exclusively takes the form of cultural hegemony in the West is a classical tenet of reformism. This is the involuntary temptation that lurks in some of Gramsci's notes. Is it truly banished by his alternative assertion that the hegemony of the Western bourgeoisie is a combination of consent and coercion? There is no doubt that this is an improvement, but the relationship between the two terms cannot be grasped by their mere conjunction or addition. Yet within Gramsci's framework everything depends on an accurate calibration of precisely this relation. How should it be conceived, theoretically?

No adequate answer to the question can be presented here. For a serious solution of it is only possible through historical enquiry. No philological commentary, or theoretical fiat, can settle the difficult problems of bourgeois class power in the West. A directly substantive and comparative investigation of the actual political systems of the major imperialist countries in the twentieth century can alone establish the real structures of the rule of capital. All that can be attempted here is to advance certain critical suggestions within the textual limits of Gramsci's discourse. Their verification necessarily remains subject to the ordinary disciplines of scientific study.

To formulate a preliminary response, we can turn to a phrase of Gramsci himself. In the first notebook he composed in prison, he referred in passing to 'forms of mixed struggle' that were 'fundamentally military and preponderantly political' in character—noting at the same time that 'every political struggle always has a military substratum'.[2] The paradoxical juxtaposition and distinction of 'fundamental' and 'preponderant' to describe the relationship between two forms of struggle, provides a formula that can be adapted for a more adequate account of the dispositions of bourgeois class power in advanced capitalism. The Althusserian tradition was later to codify the same duality with its distinction between 'determinant' and 'dominant'—taken not from Gramsci, but from Marx. In analysing the contemporary social formations of the West, we can substitute 'coercion' or 'repression' for Gramsci's 'military struggle'—as the mode of class rule enforced by violence; 'culture' or 'ideology' for his 'political struggle'—as the mode of class rule secured by consent. It is then possible to capture something like the real nature of the relationship between the two variables by which Gramsci was haunted. If we revert to Gramsci's original problematic, the normal structure of capitalist political power in bourgeois-democratic states is in effect simultaneously and indivisibly dominated by culture and determined by coercion. To deny the 'preponderant' or dominant role of culture in the contemporary bourgeois power system is to liquidate the most

2    QC I, p. 123; SPN, p. 230.

salient immediate difference between Western parliamentarism and Russian absolutism, and to reduce the former to a myth. The fact is that this cultural domination is embodied in certain irrefutably concrete institutions: regular elections, civic freedoms, rights of assembly—all of which exist in the West and none of which directly threaten the class power of capital.[3] The day-to-day system of bourgeois rule is thus based on the consent of the masses, in the form of the ideological belief that they exercise self-government in the representative state. At the same time, however, to forget the 'fundamental' or determinant role of violence within the power structure of contemporary capitalism in the final instance is to regress to reformism, in the illusion that an electoral majority can legislate socialism peacefully from a parliament.

An analogy may serve to illuminate the relationship in question—provided its limits (those of any analogy) are kept in mind. A classical monetary system was constituted from two distinct media of exchange: paper and gold.[4] It was not a

---

3    These formulations deliberately remain within the purview of Gramsci's concepts. They involve one major simplification, characteristic of the *Prison Notebooks*—the elision of the 'cultural' and 'political' dimensions of popular consent to the rule of capital. The two cannot, however, be straightforwardly equated. No bourgeois parliament was ever merely a secular simulacrum of a religious church. (See footnote at p. 65 above.) It can be said that Gramsci's attention always tended more towards the purely cultural institutions for securing the consent of the masses—churches, schools, newspapers and so on—than to the specifically political institutions which assure the stability of capitalism, with their necessarily greater complexity and ambiguity. For the purposes of the argument above, the indeterminacy characteristic of Gramsci's discussions of consent has been retained.

4    Talcott Parsons, with a characteristic mélange of insight and confusion, once advanced a comparison between power and money of a very different sort, mystifying any analogy by drawing the inimitable conclusion that a 'democratic political system' can increase the total amount of classless

summation of these two forms, for the value of fiduciary issue
which circulated every day and maintained the system under
normal conditions was dependent on the quantum of metal in
the bank reserves at any given moment, despite the fact that
this metal was virtually absent from the system as a medium
of exchange. Only the paper, not the gold, appeared within circulation, yet the paper was in the final instance determined by
the gold, without which it ceased to be sound currency. Crisis
conditions, moreover, would necessarily trigger a sudden reversion of the total system to the metal which lay invisibly behind
it: a collapse of credit infallibly produced a rush to gold.[5] In the
political system, a similar structural (non-additive and non-
transitive) relationship between ideology and repression—
consent and coercion—prevails. The normal conditions of
ideological subordination of the masses—the day-to-day rou-
tines of a parliamentary democracy—are themselves constituted
by a silent, absent force which gives them their currency: the
monopoly of legitimate violence by the state. Deprived of this,
the system of cultural control would be instantly fragile, since
the limits of possible actions against it would disappear.[6] With

---

'power' in a society by 'votes' in the same way that a banking system can
increase purchasing power by 'credit' (votes do 'double duty', like dollars
in a bank, in his phrase). See 'On the Concept of Political Power', *Proceed-
ings of the American Philosophical Society*, June 1963, now republished in
*Sociological Theory and Modern Society*, New York 1967.

5  Or to stronger foreign currencies, with a superior ratio to gold.
6  A classical example of such a sudden disappearance of 'limits' is provided
by the commentaries and refutations inserted by typographical workers
in bourgeois newspapers during a revolutionary situation. In Russia and
Cuba alike, compositors retorted to the propaganda of the capitalist press
in its own pages, by appending what the Cuban workers called 'tails' to the
more mendacious articles contained in it. The cultural control system was
thereby sprung into the air the moment the 'rights' of private property were
defied, because there was no stable state apparatus of repression to enforce

it, the system is immensely powerful—so powerful that it can, paradoxically, do 'without' it: in effect, violence may normally scarcely appear within the bounds of the system at all.

In the most tranquil democracies today, the army may remain invisible in its barracks, the police appear uncontentious on its beat. The analogy holds too in another respect. Just as gold as a material substratum of paper is itself a convention that needs acceptance as a medium of exchange, so repression as a guarantor of ideology itself depends on the assent of those who are trained to exercise it. Given this critical proviso, however, the 'fundamental' resort of bourgeois class power, beneath the 'preponderant' cusp of culture in a parliamentary system, remains coercion.

For historically, and this is the most essential point of all, the development of any revolutionary crisis necessarily displaces the dominance within the bourgeois power structure from ideology to violence. Coercion becomes both determinant and dominant in the supreme crisis, and the army inevitably occupies

---

them. Trotsky commented on this structural relationship, in his account of the situation in Russia after the February Revolution: 'How about the force of property? said the petty-bourgeois socialists, answering the Bolsheviks. Property is a relation among people. It represents an enormous power so long as it is universally acknowledged and supported by that system of compulsion called Law and the State. But the very essence of the present situation was that the old State had suddenly collapsed, and the entire old system of rights had been called into question by the masses. In the factories the workers were more and more regarding themselves as proprietors, and the bosses as uninvited guests. Still less assured were the feelings of the landlords in the provinces, face to face with those surly vengeful *muzhiks*, and far from that governmental power in whose existence they did for a time, owing to their distance from the capital, believe. The property-holders, deprived of the possibility of using their property, or protecting it, ceased to be real property-holders and became badly frightened philistines who could not give any support to the government for the simple reason that they needed it themselves.' *History of the Russian Revolution*, I, p. 197.

the front of the stage in any class struggle against the prospect of a real inauguration of socialism. Capitalist power can in this sense be regarded as a topological system with a 'mobile' centre: in any crisis, an objective redeployment occurs, and capital re-concentrates from its representative into its repressive apparatuses. The fact that the subjectivity of leading cadres of these apparatuses in Western countries today may remain innocent of any such scenario is not proof of their constitutional neutrality, but merely of the remoteness of the prospect to them. In fact, any revolutionary crisis within an advanced capitalist country must inevitably produce a reversion to the ultimate determinant of the power system: force. This is a law of capitalism, which it cannot violate, on pain of death. It is the rule of the end-game situation.

It should now be clear why Gramsci's concept of hegemony, for all its merits as a first theoretical 'divining-rod' of the uncharted specificity of Western social formations,[7] contains a potential political danger. It has been seen how the term, which originated in Russia to define the relationship between the proletariat and peasantry in a bourgeois revolution, was transferred by Gramsci to describe the relationship between the bourgeoisie and proletariat in a consolidated capitalist order in Western Europe. The common thread which permitted this extension was the consensual tenor of the idea of hegemony. Used in Russia to denote the persuasive nature of the influence the working class should seek to win over the peasantry, as opposed to the coercive nature of the struggle to overthrow Tsarism, it was then applied by Gramsci to the forms of consent to its rule won by

---

7   The greatest achievement of Gramsci's thought in prison—his theory of intellectuals, which produced the most sustained single text in the *Notebooks*—is perforce omitted altogether from this essay. Suffice it to say that in this field, Gramsci's historical exploration of the complexities of European societies had, and has, no equal within Marxism.

the bourgeoisie from the working class in the West. The service which he rendered to Marxism, by focusing so centrally on the—hitherto evaded—problem of the consensual legitimacy of parliamentary institutions in Western Europe, was a solitary and signal one. At the same time, however, the risks attendant on the new extension of the concept of hegemony were soon evident in his writings.

For whereas in Russia the term could exhaust the relationship between proletariat and peasantry, since the former was an alliance between non-antagonistic classes, the same could never be true in, say, Italy or France of the relationship between bourgeoisie and proletariat—inherently a conflict between antagonistic classes, founded on two adversary positions within the capitalist mode of production. In other words, capitalist rule in the West necessarily comprised coercion as well as consent. Gramsci's awareness of this was expressed in the numerous formulations in his notebooks which refer to the combinations between the two. But, as we have seen, these never succeed in locating definitely or precisely either the position or the interconnexion of repression and ideology within the power structure of advanced capitalism. Moreover, in so far as Gramsci at times suggested that consent primarily pertained to civil society, and civil society possessed primacy over the state, he allowed the conclusion that bourgeois class power was primarily consensual. In this form, the idea of hegemony tends to accredit the notion that the dominant mode of bourgeois power in the West—'culture'—is also the determinant mode, either by suppressing the latter or fusing the two modes together. It thereby omits the unappealable role in the last instance of force.

However, Gramsci's use of the term hegemony was not, of course, confined to the bourgeoisie as a social class. He also employed it to trace the paths of ascent of the proletariat in the West. A further shift in the evolution of the concept was involved here. The prescriptive relationship proletariat/peasantry had plausibly been equated with a cultural ascendancy; the actual relationship bourgeoisie/proletariat certainly included a cultural ascendancy, although it could not be equated or reduced to it; but could the relationship proletariat/bourgeoisie be said in any sense to betoken or promise a cultural ascendancy? Many admirers of Gramsci have thought so. Indeed, it has often been held that his most original and powerful single thesis was precisely the idea that the working class can be hegemonic culturally before becoming the ruling class politically, within a capitalist social formation. Official interpretations of Gramsci have, in particular, been keyed to such a prospect. The text from the *Prison Notebooks* to which reference is customarily made does not, however, assert this. In it, Gramsci wrote: 'A social group is dominant over enemy groups which it tends to "liquidate" or subject with armed force, and is directive over affinal and allied groups. A social group can and indeed must be directive before conquering governmental power (this is one of the main conditions for the conquest of power itself); afterwards, when it exercises power and keeps it firmly in its grasp, it becomes dominant but also continues to be "directive".'[8] Gramsci here carefully distinguishes the necessity for coercion of enemy classes from the consensual direction of allied classes. The 'hegemonic activity' which 'can and must be exercised before the assumption of power' is related in this context only to the problem of the alliances of the working class with other exploited and oppressed groups; it is not a claim to hegemony over the whole of society, or the ruling class itself, by definition impossible at this stage.

---

8    *QC* III, pp. 2010–11; *SPN*, pp. 57–8.

It is true, however, that any unwary reader can be led to mis-construe this passage, where Gramsci is actually on safe ground, by ambiguities in his use of the term hegemony elsewhere. We shall see why shortly. For the moment, what is important to recall is the familiar Marxist tenet that the working class under capitalism is inherently incapable of being the cultur-ally dominant class, because it is structurally expropriated by its class position from some of the essential means of cultural production (education, tradition, leisure)—in contrast to the bourgeoisie of the Enlightenment, which could generate its own superior culture within the framework of the Ancien Régime. Not only this, but even after a socialist revolution—the conquest of political power by the proletariat—the culturally dominant class remains the bourgeoisie in certain respects (not all—habits more than ideas) and for a certain time (in principle shorter with each revolution), as Lenin and Trotsky emphasised in different contexts.[9] Gramsci was intermittently conscious of this too.[10] So long, however, as the lack of structural correspondence between the positions of the bourgeois class within feudal society and the working class within capitalist society was not constantly

---

9    Lenin, *Collected Works*, Vol. 28, pp. 252–3; Trotsky, *Literature and Revolu-tion*, Michigan 1966, pp. 184–200.

10   Thus in one fragment he argued that in the necessary absence of cultural superiority, the working class would initially have to rely to excess on politi-cal command, producing the phenomenon of what he called statolatry. 'For some social groups, which before their ascent to autonomous State life have not had a long independent period of cultural and moral development on their own (such as was made possible in mediaeval society and under the Absolute regimes by the juridical existence of privileged Estates or orders), a period of statolatry is necessary and indeed opportune. This "statolatry" is nothing other than the normal form of "State life", or at least initiation to autonomous State life and the creation of a "civil society" which it was not historically possible to create before the ascent to independent State life.' *QC* II, p. 1020; *SPN*, p. 268.

registered, the risk of a theoretical slide from one to the other was always potentially present in the common use of the term hegemony for them. The more than occasional assimilation of the bourgeois and proletarian revolutions in his writings on Jacobinism demonstrates that Gramsci was not immune to this confusion. The result was to permit later codifications of his thought to link his two extensions of the concept of hegemony into a classically reformist syllogism. For once bourgeois power in the West is primarily attributed to cultural hegemony, the acquisition of this hegemony would mean effective assumption by the working class of the 'direction of society' without the seizure and transformation of state power, in a painless transition to socialism: in other words, a typical idea of Fabianism. Gramsci himself, of course, never drew this conclusion. But in the scattered letter of his texts, it was not an entirely arbitrary interpolation either.

How was it possible for Gramsci, a communist militant with a past of unwavering—indeed undue—political hostility to reformism, to leave a legacy of such ambiguity? The answer must be sought in the framework of reference within which he wrote. The theory and practice of the Third International, from the inception of its history with Lenin to the incarceration of Gramsci, had been saturated with emphasis on the historical necessity of violence in the destruction and construction of states. The dictatorship of the proletariat, after the armed overthrow of the bourgeois state apparatus, was the touchstone —tirelessly proclaimed in every official document—of the Marxism of the Comintern. Gramsci never questioned these principles. On the contrary, when he started his theoretical explorations in prison, he seems to have taken them so much for granted that they scarcely ever figure directly in his discourse at all. They form as it were the familiar acquisition, which no longer needed reiteration, in an intellectual enterprise whose energies were concentrated elsewhere—on the discovery of the unfamiliar. But in the absence of any possibility of integrated composition, denied him in prison, Gramsci's intent pursuit of new themes and ideas exposed him to the persistent risk of temporarily losing sight of older verities, and so of neglecting or mistaking the relationship between the two. The problem of consent, which forms the real fulcrum of his work, is the critical point of this process. Gramsci was acutely aware of the novelty and difficulty for Marxist theory of the phenomenon of institutionalised popular consent to capital in the West—hitherto regularly evaded or repressed within the Comintern tradition. He therefore focussed all the powers of his intelligence on it. In doing so, he never intended to deny or rescind the classical axioms of that tradition on the inevitable role of social coercion within any great historical transformation, so long as classes subsisted. His objective was, in one of his phrases, to 'complement' treatment of the one with an exploration of the other.

The premises and aims that produced the selective lens of his work can be seen with particular clarity in his commentaries on Croce. The importance of Croce for Gramsci's whole programme in prison is well known. His remarks on Croce's historical studies are therefore especially revealing. Gramsci repeatedly and expressly criticised Croce for his unilateral exaltation of the consensual and moral, and concomitant evasion of the military and coercive, moments in European history. 'In his two recent books, *The History of Italy* and *The History of Europe*, it is precisely the moments of force, of struggle, of misery that are omitted ... Is it an accident, or is it tendentiously, that Croce starts his narratives from 1815 and 1871 respectively?

In other words, that he excludes the moment of struggle, the moment in which conflicting forces are formed, assembled and deployed, the moment in which one system of social relations dissolves and another is forged in fire and steel, the moment in which one system of social relations disintegrates and declines while another emerges and affirms itself—and instead placidly assumes the moment of cultural or ethico-political expansion to be all history?'[11]

The terse terms of Gramsci's summary of the political bent of Crocean idealist historiography show how naturally he assumed the classical canons of revolutionary Marxism. 'Ethico-political history is an arbitrary and mechanical hypostasis of the moment of hegemony, of political direction, of consent, in the life and in the development of the State and of civil society.'[12] Yet at the same time, Gramsci regarded Croce as a superior thinker to Gentile, who committed the opposite hypostasis—a fetishism of force and state—in his philosophy of actualism. 'For Gentile, history is exclusively history of the State. For Croce it is rather "ethico-political", that is Croce wants to preserve a distinction between civil society and political society, between hegemony and dictatorship; great intellectuals exercise hegemony, which presupposes a certain collaboration, in other words an active and voluntary (free) consent, in a liberal-democratic order. Gentile poses the economico-corporative phase as the ethical phase in the act of history: hegemony and dictatorship are indistinguishable, force is consent without further ado: political society cannot be differentiated from civil society: the State alone exists, and naturally as the government State.'[13]

---

11   *QC* II, p. 1316; *QC* II, p. 1227; *SPN*, p. 119.
12   *QC* II, p. 1222.
13   *QC* II, p. 691; *SPN*, p. 271.

For in fact, with all its exaggeration, it was precisely Croce's emphasis on the role of culture and the significance of consent that was the reason for the pre-eminent theoretical status Gramsci attributed to him. To Gramsci, these represented a philosophical exordium or equivalent to the doctrine of hegemony within historical materialism. 'Croce's thought should therefore at the very least be appreciated as an instrumental value, for it can be said that he has energetically drawn attention to the importance of the phenomena of culture and of thought in the development of history, of the function of major intellectuals in the organic life of civil society and the State, of the moment of hegemony and consent in the necessary form of any concrete historical bloc.'[14] Thus Croce could even be compared by Gramsci to Lenin, as joint authors of the notion of hegemony: 'Contemporaneously with Croce, the greatest modern theorist of Marxism has, on the terrain of political organisation and struggle, and in political terminology, revalued—in opposition to diverse "economist" tendencies—the doctrine of hegemony as the complement to the theory of the State as coercion.'[15]

In his final assessment, Gramsci was so seized with the importance of Croce's 'ethico-political history' that he could argue that Marxism as a philosophy could only achieve a modern renewal through a critique and integration of Croce, comparable to Marx's assimilation and supersession of Hegel. In his famous dictum: 'It is necessary for us to repeat today the same reduction of Croce's philosophy as the first theorists of Marxism accomplished for Hegel's philosophy. This is the sole historically fecund way of achieving an adequate renewal of Marxism, of elevating

---

14  *QC* II, p. 1235.
15  *QC* II, p. 1235. See also *Lettere dal Carcere*, p. 616, for the same comparison.

its conceptions—perforce "vulgarised" in immediate practical life—to the heights necessary for it to be able to resolve the more complex tasks of the present development of struggle—that is, the creation of an integral new culture, which would have the popular characteristics of the Protestant Reformation and the French Enlightenment, and the classical traits of Greek culture and of the Italian Renaissance, a culture which would—in Carducci's phrase—synthesise Maximilien Robespierre and Immanuel Kant, politics and philosophy in a single dialectical unity, belonging to a social group that was not merely French or German, but European and universal. The heritage of German classical philosophy must not merely be inventoried, but made to live actively again. For that, it is necessary to come to terms with the philosophy of Croce.'[16] The curvature of Gramsci's comments on Croce thus traces very accurately the way in which he presumed the gains of the Comintern tradition; preferred to explore what it had relatively neglected; and ended by overstating the case for a bourgeois tradition that had not done so, whose weaknesses he had started by criticizing.

The inadvertent movement of thought visible in these texts on Croce was responsible for the paradoxes of Gramsci's theorisation of hegemony. To understand them, it is necessary to separate the objective logic of Gramsci's terms from his subjective political stance as a whole. For the involuntary concatenation of the one yielded results in profound contradiction with the inmost will of the other. The disjuncture that silently developed in Gramsci's notebooks was due, of course, to his inability to write any ordinary statement of his overall views. In this sense,

---

16   *QC* II, p. 1223. Elsewhere, Gramsci compared Croce—'the greatest Italian prose-writer since Manzoni'—to Goethe, for his 'serenity, composure and imperturbability.' *Lettere dal Carcere*, p. 612.

fascist censorship, while not preventing his research, exacted an undeniable toll on it. Throughout his imprisonment, Gramsci wrestled with the relations between coercion and consent in the advanced capitalist societies of the West. But because he could never produce a unitary theory of the two—which would necessarily have had to take the form of a direct and comprehensive survey of the intricate institutional patterns of bourgeois power, in either their parliamentary or their fascist variants—an unwitting list gradually edged his texts towards the pole of consent, at the expense of that of coercion.

The conceptual slippage which results in Gramsci's work can be compared with that which marks the thought of his celebrated ancestor and inspiration in prison. For Machiavelli, from whom Gramsci took so many themes, had also set out to analyse the dual forms of the Centaur—half-man, half-beast—symbol of the hybrid of compulsion and consent by which men were always governed. In Machiavelli's work, however, the slide occurred in exactly the opposite direction. Ostensibly concerned with 'arms' and 'laws', coercion and consent, his actual discourse slipped unstoppably towards 'force' and 'fraud'—in other words, the animal component of power alone.[17] The result was the rhetoric of repression later generations were to call Machiavellianism. Gramsci adopted Machiavelli's myth of the Centaur as the emblematic motto of his research: but where Machiavelli had effectively collapsed consent into coercion, in Gramsci

---

17  For an analysis of the sliding structures of Machiavelli's thought, and their relation to the political setting of Renaissance Italy, see *Lineages of the Absolute State*, pp. 163–8. The dualist cast of Gramsci's political theory descended directly from Machiavelli, for whom 'arms' and 'laws' were naturally exhaustive of power—two centuries before the emergence of economic theory in Europe, and three before the advent of historical materialism. Gramsci's return to the voluntarist categories of the Renaissance necessarily bypassed the problem of economic constraints.

coercion was progressively eclipsed by consent. *The Prince* and *The Modern Prince* are in this sense distorting mirrors of each other. There is an inverse correspondence between the failings of the two.

We may now recollect the famous comparison between East and West in the *Prison Notebooks*, with which we started. Gramsci defined the contrast between the two in terms of the relative position occupied by state and civil society in each. In Russia, the state was 'everything', while civil society was 'primordial and gelatinous'. In Western Europe, on the contrary, the state was merely an 'outer ditch', while civil society was a 'powerful system of fortresses and earthworks' whose complex structures could withstand seismic political or economic crises for the state. These texts of Gramsci, which seek to capture the strategic differences between Russia and the West for a socialist revolution, set him apart from his contemporaries. In the immediate aftermath of the October Revolution, there were many socialists in Central and Western Europe who sensed that the local conditions in which they had to fight were far from those which had obtained in Russia, and who initially said so.[18] None, however, provided any coherent analysis or serious explanation of the fateful divergence in the historical experience of the European working class of the time. By the end of the twenties, the problem of the contrast between Russia and the West had effectively disappeared from Marxist debate. With the Stalinisation of the Comintern, and the institutionalisation of what was presented as an official Leninism within it, the example of the USSR became the mandatory paradigm for all issues of revolutionary theory and practice to militants across Europe. Gramsci was unique among Communists in persisting, at the nadir of the defeats of

---

18 Lukács and Gorter were examples, among others.

the thirties, to see that Russian experience could not be merely repeated in the West, and in trying to understand why. No other thinker in the European working class movement has to this day addressed himself so deeply or centrally to the problem of the specificity of a socialist revolution in the West.

Yet, for all the intensity and originality of his enquiry, Gramsci never finally succeeded in arriving at an adequate Marxist account of the distinction between East and West. The image from the compass itself proved, in the end, a snare. For a simple geographical opposition includes by definition an unproblematic comparability of the two terms. Transferred to social formations, however, it implies something that can never be taken for granted: that there is a straightforward historical comparability between them. In other words, the terms East and West assume that the social formations on each side of the divide exist in the same temporality, and can therefore be read off against each other as variations of a common category. It is this unspoken presupposition which lies behind the central texts of Gramsci's notebooks. His whole contrast between Russia and Western Europe revolves on the difference in the relationship between state and civil society in the two zones: its unexamined premise is that the state is the same type of object in both. But this assumption was just what needed to be questioned.

For, in fact, there was no initial unity to found a simple distinction between East and West of the sort that Gramsci was seeking. In its nature and structure, the Tsarism of Nicholas II was a specifically 'Eastern' variant of a feudal state, whose Western counterparts—the Absolute monarchies of France or England, Spain or Sweden—had died out centuries before.[19]

---

19  For a full-length discussion, see *Lineages of the Absolutist State*, pp. 345–60.

In other words, the constant comparison between the Russian and Western States was a paralogism, unless the differential historical time of each was specified. A prior comprehension of the uneven development of European feudalism was thus a necessary preamble to a Marxist definition of the Tsarist state which was finally destroyed by the first socialist revolution. For it alone could yield the theoretical concept of absolutism that would allow socialist militants to see the enormous gulf between the Russian autocracy and the capitalist states with which they were confronted in the West (and whose theoretical concept had to be constructed separately).

The representative state which had gradually emerged in Western Europe, North America and Japan, after the complex chain of bourgeois revolutions whose final episodes dated only from the late nineteenth century, was still a largely uncharted political object for Marxists when the Bolshevik Revolution occurred. In the early years of the Third International, the light of October blinded many revolutionaries outside Russia to the nature of their national enemy altogether. Those who remained lucid initially tried to adapt to their indigenous realities without relinquishing their fidelity to the cause of the Russian Revolution, by evoking the difference between East and West. They soon desisted. Gramsci alone, isolated from the Comintern, took up this path again and pursued it with matchless courage in prison. But so long as the simultaneity of its terms was assumed, the conundrum of the difference was ultimately unanswerable. The failure to produce a focussed comparative analysis of the respective types of state and structures of power in Russia and the West was in no way peculiar to Gramsci. From the other side of the continental divide, no Bolshevik leader succeeded in developing a coherent theory of it either. The true contrast between the

Tsarist and the Western states eluded each from opposite ends. Thus Lenin never mistook the class character of Tsarism: he always expressly insisted, against Menshevik opponents, that Russian absolutism was a feudal state machine.[20] Yet he also never adequately or systematically contrasted the parliamentary states of the West with the autocratic state in the East. There is no direct theory of bourgeois democracy anywhere in his writings. Gramsci, on the other hand, was intensely conscious of the novelty of the capitalist state in the West, as an object for Marxist analysis and adversary for Marxist strategy, and of the integrity of representative institutions to its normal operation. He, however, never perceived that the absolutism in Russia with which he contrasted it was a feudal state—a political edifice of a different order altogether. In the no man's land between the thought of the two, revolutionary socialism missed a theoretical junction critical for its future in Europe.

In the case of Gramsci, his inability to grasp the historical disjuncture concealed by the geographical form of his unity-distinction left its determinate effects on his theory of bourgeois power in the West. Gramsci, as we have seen, was constantly aware of the twin character of this power, but he never succeeded in giving it a stable formulation. Thus his passages on the distinction between East and West all suffer from the same flaw; their ultimate logic is always to tend to revert to the simple schema of an opposition between 'hegemony' (consent) in the West and 'dictatorship' (coercion) in the East: parliamentarism versus Tsarism. In Tsarist Russia, 'there was no legal political freedom, nor any religious freedom either,'[21] within a state that left no

20  Lenin, *Collected Works*, Vol. 17, pp. 114–15, 146, 153, 187, 233–41; Vol. 18, pp. 70–77; Vol. 24, pp. 44,
21  *QC* III, p. 1666.

autonomy to civil society. In Republican France, by contrast, 'the parliamentary regime realised the permanent hegemony of the urban class over the population as a whole' by means of 'rule by permanently organised consent', in which 'the organisation of consent is left to private initiatives, and is thus moral or ethical in character, because it is in one way or another "voluntarily" given'.[22] The weakness of Gramsci's counterposition was not so much its overestimation of the ideological claims of the Tsarist state within the Russian social formation—which was indeed far more extensive than that of any contemporary Western state, if not as absolute as Gramsci's attribution to it of a command over 'everything'. It was its underestimation of the specificity and stability of the repressive machinery of army and police, and its functional relationship to the representative machinery of suffrage and parliament, within the Western state.

Strangely, it was not Gramsci but his comrade and antagonist Amadeo Bordiga who was to formulate the true nature of the distinction between East and West, although he never theorised it into any cogent political practice. At the fateful Sixth Plenum of the Executive Committee of the Communist International, in February–March 1926, Bordiga—by now isolated and suspected within his own party—confronted Stalin and Bukharin for the final time. In a remarkable speech to the Plenum, he said:

> We have in the International only one party that has achieved revolutionary victory—the Bolshevik Party. They say that we should therefore take the road which led the Russian party to success. This is perfectly true, but it remains insufficient. The fact is that the Russian party fought under special conditions, in a country where the bourgeois-liberal revolution had not yet been accomplished and

---

22  *QC* III, p. 1636; *SPN*, p. 80n.

the feudal aristocracy had not yet been defeated by the capitalist bourgeoisie. Between the fall of the feudal autocracy and the seizure of power by the working class lay too short a period for there to be any comparison with the development which the proletariat will have to accomplish in other countries. For there was no time to build a bourgeois State machine on the ruins of the Tsarist feudal apparatus. Russian development does not provide us with an experience of how the proletariat can overthrow a liberal-parliamentary capitalist State that has existed for many years and possesses the ability to defend itself. We, however, must know how to attack a modern bourgeois-democratic State that on the one hand has its own means of ideologically mobilizing and corrupting the proletariat, and on the other can defend itself on the terrain of armed struggle with greater efficacy than could the Tsarist autocracy. This problem never arose in the history of the Russian Communist Party.[23]

Here the real opposition between Russia and the West emerges clearly and unambiguously: feudal autocracy against bourgeois democracy. The accuracy of Bordiga's formulation allowed him to grasp the essential twin character of the capitalist state: it was stronger than the Tsarist state, because it rested not only on the consent of the masses, but also on a superior repressive apparatus. In other words, it is not the mere 'extent' of the state that defines its location in the structure of power (what Gramsci elsewhere called 'statolatry'), but also its efficacy. The repressive apparatus of any modern capitalist state is inherently superior to that of Tsarism, for two reasons. Firstly, because the Western

---

23  *Protokoll der Erweiterten Exekutive der Kommunistischen Internationale,* February–March 1926, Hamburg 1926, p. 126. Note that the French version of this speech in *Correspondence Internationale,* 13 March 1926, was much abridged. Bordiga went on to make an eloquent indictment of the demagogic ouvrierism and organisational inquisitions under way in the Third International by that date.

social formations are much more industrially advanced, and this technology is reflected in the apparatus of violence itself. Secondly, because the masses typically consent to this state in the belief that they exercise government over it. It therefore possesses a popular legitimacy of a far more reliable character for the exercise of this repression than did Tsarism in its decline, reflected in the greater discipline and loyalty of its troops and police—juridically the servants, not of an irresponsible autocrat, but of an elected assembly. The keys to the power of the capitalist state in the West lie in this conjoined superiority.

# 4

# CONTEXTS

We can now, in conclusion, review Gramsci's strategic doctrine—in other words, the political perspectives that he deduced from his theoretical analysis of the nature of bourgeois rule in the West. What were the lessons of the morphology of capitalist hegemony, as he sought to reconstruct it in prison, for the working class movement? What was the political crux of the problem of the bourgeois state for a Western strategy of the proletarian revolution? Gramsci, as a theorist and a militant, never separated the two. His solution to the cipher of success in the West was, as we have seen, a 'war of position'. What was the real meaning and effect of this formula?

To understand Gramsci's strategic theory, it is necessary to retrace the decisive original polemic within the European workers' movement to which it was a hidden, ulterior response. With the victory of the Russian Revolution, and the collapse of the Hohenzollern and Habsburg empires in central Europe, key theorists of German communism came to believe that, in the aftermath of the First World War, the seizure of power by the proletariat was on the immediate agenda in every imperialist country, because the world had now definitively entered the historical epoch of the socialist revolution. This belief was most fully and forcefully expressed by Georg Lukács, then a leading member of the exiled Hungarian Communist Party, writing in the German-language theoretical review *Kommunismus* in Vienna. For Lukács, there was now a 'universal actuality of the proletarian revolution', determined by the general stage of the development of capitalism, which was henceforward in mortal crisis.

> 'This means that the actuality of the revolution is no longer only a world-historical horizon arching over the self-liberating working class, but that revolution is already on its agenda ... The actuality of the revolution provides the key-note of the whole epoch.'[1]

This fusion—confusion—between the theoretical concepts of historical epoch and historical conjuncture allowed Lukács and prominent colleagues in the KPD such as Thalheimer and Frölich to ignore the problem of the concrete preconditions for a revolutionary situation by abstractly affirming the revolutionary character of the time itself. On this premise, they went on to argue for a novel tactic: the *Teilaktion* or 'partial' armed action against the capitalist state.

Within the ranks of the Second International, Bernstein and co-thinkers had maintained the possibility of 'partial' ameliorations of capitalism by means of parliamentary reforms, that would in a gradual process of evolution eventually lead to the peaceful completion of socialism. The illusion that the inherent unity of the capitalist state could be divided or attained by successive partial measures, slowly transforming its class character, had been a traditional prerogative of reformism. There now,

---

1   Georg Lukács, *Lenin*, London 1970, p. 12.

however, emerged an adventurist version of the same error in the Third International. For in 1920–21, Thalheimer, Frölich, Lukács and others theorised putschist 'partial actions' as a series of armed attacks against the bourgeois state, limited in scope yet constant in tempo. In the words of *Kommunismus*: 'The principal characteristic of the present period of the revolution lies in this, that we are now compelled to conduct even partial battles, including economic ones, with the instrumentalities of the final battle', above all 'armed insurrection'.[2]

This was the theory of the 'revolutionary offensive'. Since the epoch was revolutionary, the only correct strategy was an offensive one, to be mounted in a series of repeated armed blows against the capitalist state. These should be undertaken even if the working class was not in an immediately revolutionary mood: they would then precisely serve to 'awaken' the proletariat from its reformist torpor. Lukács provided the most sophisticated justification of these adventures. He argued that partial actions were not so much 'organisational measures by which the Communist Party could seize State power' as 'autonomous and active initiatives of the KPD to overcome the ideological crisis and menshevik lethargy of the proletariat, and standstill of revolutionary development'.[3] For Lukács, the rationale of the *Teilaktionen* was thus not their objective aims, but their subjective impact on the consciousness of the working class. 'If revolutionary development is not to run the risk of stagnation, another outcome must be found: the action of the KPD in an offensive. An offensive signifies: the independent action of

---

2    '*Der Krise der Kommunistischen Internationale und der Dritte Kongress*', Editorial in *Kommunismus*, 15 June 1921, p. 691.
3    '*Spontaneität der Massen, Aktivität der Partei*', *Die Internationale*, III 8, 1921, pp. 213–14. For an English text, see Georg Lukács, *Political Writings 1919–1929*, London 1972, p. 102.

the party at the right moment with the right slogan, to awaken the proletarian masses from their inertia, to wrest them away from their menshevik leadership by action (in other words organisationally and not merely ideologically), and thereby to cut the knot of the ideological crisis of the proletariat with the sword of the deed.'[4]

The fate of these pronouncements was rapidly settled by the lesson of events themselves. The radical misunderstanding of the integral unity of capitalist state power, and the necessarily all-or-nothing character of any insurrection against it, naturally led to disaster in Central Germany. In March 1921, the KPD launched its much vaunted offensive against the Prussian state government, by falling into the trap of a badly prepared rising against a preventive police occupation of the Mansfeld–Merseburg area. In the absence of any spontaneous working class resistance, the KPD desperately resorted to dynamiting actions designed to provoke police bombardments; seizure of factories and street fighting followed; wandering guerrilla bands submerged any discipline in anarchic forays through the countryside. For a week, heavy fighting raged in Central Germany between KPD militants and the police and Reichswehr units mobilised to suppress them. The result was a foregone conclusion. Isolated from the rest of the German proletariat, bewildered and dislocated by the arbitrary character of the action, hopelessly outnumbered by the concentration of Reichswehr troops in the Merseburg–Halle region, the vanguard flung into this confrontation with the full might of the army was routed. A drastic wave of repression succeeded the March Action. Some 4,000 militants were sentenced to prison, and the KPD received its quietus in Prussian Saxony.

---

4   '*Spontaneität der Massen, Aktivität der Partei*', p. 215; *Political Writings*, p. 104.

Not only was the objective of state power never achieved, but the subjective impact on the German working class and the KPD itself was calamitous. Far from rousing the proletariat from its 'menshevik lethargy', the March Action demoralised and disillusioned it. The vanguard zone of the Merseburg mines relapsed into a desert of apolitical backwardness. Worse still, the KPD never wholly regained the trust of wide sections of the German proletariat thereafter. Its membership had been 350,000 before the March offensive: within a few weeks of the disaster, it had plummeted to half that number. It never attained comparable levels of strength again in the Weimar Republic.

The adventurism of the KPD in 1921 was condemned by the Third World Congress of the Comintern. Lenin wrote a famous letter to the German Party, demolishing the justifications for it. Trotsky denounced the whole theory of *Teilaktion*: 'A purely mechanical conception of the proletarian revolution—which proceeds solely from the fact that the capitalist economy continues to decay—has led certain groups of comrades to construe theories which are false to the core: the false theory of an initiating minority which by its heroism shatters "the wall of universal passivity" among the proletariat, the false theory of uninterrupted offensives conducted by the proletarian vanguard as a "new method" of struggle, the false theory of partial battles which are waged by applying the methods of armed insurrection and so on. The clearest exponent of this is the Vienna journal *Kommunismus*. It is absolutely self-evident that tactical theories of this sort have nothing in common with Marxism. To apply them in practice is to play directly into the hands of the bourgeoisie's military-political leaders and their strategy.'[5]

---

5    Trotsky, 'The Main Lessons of the Third Congress', in *The First Five Years of the Communist International*, I, New York 1945, pp. 295–6.

Lenin and Trotsky together waged a resolute fight against the theory of the *Teilaktion* at the Third World Congress of the Communist International, and over German opposition it was formally repudiated by the Comintern.

Against this background it is now possible to reconsider Gramsci's later attempt to define the specificity of a Western revolutionary strategy as a 'war of position'. For Gramsci's axiom was designed to represent the political correction he believed necessary after the failure of the March Action—which he saw as the expression of a 'war of manoeuvre'. His dating of the two is precise and unequivocal: 'In the present epoch, the war of movement occurred politically between March 1917 and March 1921, and it was then followed by a war of position.'[6] The contrast between war of manoeuvre and war of position, it will be remembered, was derived by analogy from the First World War. Whereas in Russia, Gramsci wrote, the revolution could make fast, mobile sorties against the state, and overthrow it at great speed, in the industrialised West such insurrectionary tactics would lead to defeat, much as the campaign of the Tsar's army in Galicia had done. 'It seems to me that Lenin understood that a change was necessary from the war of manoeuvre applied victoriously in the East in 1917, to a war of position which was the only possible form in the West—where, as Krasnov observes, armies could rapidly accumulate endless quantities of munitions, and where the social structures were of themselves still capable of becoming heavily armed fortifications. This is what the formula of the "united front" seems to me to mean.'[7]

Gramsci's explicit equation of 'united front' with 'war of position', which might otherwise seem baffling, becomes immediately

6    *QC* II, p. 1229; *SPN*, p. 120.

7    *QC* II, p. 866; *SPN*, p. 237.

clear. For the United Front was the political line adopted by the Comintern after the Third World Congress had condemned the 'theory of the offensive' advocated by the KPD—a war of manoeuvre. The strategic objective of the United Front was to win over the masses in the West to revolutionary Marxism, by patient organisation and skilful agitation for working-class unity in action. Lenin, who coined the slogan 'To the Masses' with which the Comintern Congress of 1921 closed, expressly emphasised its importance for a differential strategy adapted to countries in Western Europe, in contradistinction to those in Russia. In his speech of 1 July, replying to Terracini—the representative of Gramsci's own party, the PCI—he devoted his address precisely to this theme. 'We were victorious in Russia not only because the undisputed majority of the working class (during the elections of 1917 the overwhelming majority of the workers were with us against the Mensheviks) was on our side, but also because half the army, immediately after our seizure of power, and nine-tenths of the peasants, in the course of some weeks, came over to our side; we were victorious because we took, not our agrarian programme, but that of the Socialist-Revolutionaries and put it into effect. Our victory lay in the fact that we carried out the Socialist-Revolutionary Programme; that is why this victory was so easy. Is it possible that you in the West have such illusions (about the repeatability of this process)? It is ridiculous. Just compare the economic conditions! ... We were a small Party in Russia, but we had with us in addition the majority of the Soviets of Workers' and Peasants' Deputies throughout the country. Where do you have that? We had with us nearly half the army, which numbered at least 10 million men. Do you really have the majority of the army behind you? Show me such a country! ... Can you point to any country in Europe where you could win over the majority of the peasantry in some weeks? Perhaps Italy? (laughter)[8]

Lenin went on to stress the absolute necessity of winning the masses in the West, before any attempt to achieve power could be successful. This need not always imply the creation of a vast political party: it meant that the revolution could only be made with and by the masses themselves, who would have to be convinced of this goal by their vanguard in an extremely arduous preparatory phase of struggle. 'I am certainly not denying that revolution can be started by a very small party and brought to a victorious conclusion. But we have to know the methods by which the masses can be won over to our side ... An absolute majority is not always essential; but for victory and for retaining power, what is essential is not only the majority of the working class—I use the term working class in its West European sense, i.e. in the sense of the industrial proletariat—but also the majority of the working and exploited population. Have you thought about this?'[9]

Gramsci was thus correct in thinking that Lenin had formulated the policies of the United Front in 1921 to answer to the specific problems of revolutionary strategy in Western Europe. At the time, of course, Gramsci himself—together with nearly the whole leadership of the PCI—had stubbornly rejected the United Front in Italy, and had thereby facilitated the victory of fascism, which was able to triumph over a divided working class. From 1921 to 1924, the years when the Comintern seriously tried to secure the implementation of United Front tactics towards the PSI Maximalists in Italy, both Bordiga and Gramsci refused, resisting the line of the International. By the time

8   Lenin, *Collected Works*, Vol. 32, pp. 474–5, 471, 474.
9   Lenin, *Collected Works*, Vol. 32, p. 476.

Gramsci had assumed the leadership of the party in 1924, and rallied to a policy of fidelity to the International, fascism was already installed and the Comintern—now radically changed in character—had largely abandoned United Front tactics itself. Thus Gramsci's insistence on the concept of the 'united front' in his *Prison Notebooks* in the thirties does not represent a renewal of his political past: on the contrary, it marks a retrospective break with it.

For it was the contemporary situation in the Communist International which determined the nature and direction of the strategic texts written during Gramsci's imprisonment. In 1928, the famous Third Period of the Comintern had started. Its premise was the prediction of an immediate and catastrophic crisis of world capitalism—apparently vindicated shortly afterwards by the Great Depression. Its axioms included the identity of fascism and social democracy, the equivalence of police dictatorships and bourgeois democracies, the necessity of breakaway trade unions, and the duty of physical combat against recalcitrant workers and labour officials. This was the epoch of 'social-fascism', 'independent unions' and 'storming the streets', when left social democrats were declared the worst of all enemies of the working class, and the advent of the Nazis to power was greeted in advance as a welcome clarification of the class struggle. In these years, the Communist International plunged into an ultra-left frenzy that made the partisans of the March Action seem restrained by comparison. In Italy itself, at the height of Mussolini's power, the exiled PCI declared a revolutionary situation to be present, and the dictatorship of the proletariat the only permissible immediate goal of struggle. Socialists in common exile—whether maximalist or reformist—were denounced as agents of fascism. Wave after wave of cadres were sent into the country, only to be arrested and jailed by the secret police, while their successes were announced in official propaganda abroad.

Confronted with this general rush to disaster, in which his own party was implicated, Gramsci refused its official positions and in his search for another strategic line recalled the United Front. The reason is now easy to see: a decade earlier, the latter had been a riposte to adventurist aberrations that anticipated— in a less extreme form—those of the Third Period. The United Front acquired a new relevance for Gramsci in the conjuncture of the early thirties. Indeed, it can be said that it was the madness of the Third Period that finally helped him to understand it. His emphasis on the United Front in his *Prison Notebooks* thus has an unequivocal meaning. It is a denial that the Italian masses had abandoned social-democratic and bourgeois-democratic illusions, were in a revolutionary ferment against fascism, or could be immediately aroused to mobilise for the dictatorship of the proletariat in Italy; and an insistence that these same masses must be won over to the struggle against fascism, that working class unity could and should be achieved by pacts of action between communists and social democrats, and that the fall of fascism would not automatically be the victory of social- ism, because there was always the possibility of a restoration of parliamentarism. The United Front, in other words, signified the necessity for deep and serious ideological-political work among the masses, untainted by sectarianism, before the seizure of power could be on the agenda.

At the same time, Gramsci's strategic reorientation in prison moved beyond the conjunctural imperatives of peninsular resistance to fascism. It was Western Europe as a whole, not simply Italy, that was the spatial horizon of his political thought in these years. Similarly, it was the entire post-war epoch after

1921, not merely the darkness of the early thirties, that was its temporal reference. To convey the scope of the change in political perspective which he sought to theorise, Gramsci developed the precept of the 'war of position'. Valid for a complete era and an entire zone of social struggle, the idea of a 'war of position' thus had a much wider resonance than that of the tactic of the United Front once advocated by the Comintern. Yet it was at this delicate point of transition in Gramsci's thought, where it sought a superior strategic resolution, that it ran into jeopardy.

For, unknown to himself, Gramsci had an illustrious predecessor. Karl Kautsky, in a famous debate with Rosa Luxemburg, had in 1910 argued that the German working class in its fight against capital should adopt an *Ermattungsstrategie*—a 'strategy of attrition'. He explicitly counterposed this conception to what he called a *Niederwerfungsstrategie*—a 'strategy of overthrow'. Kautsky did not coin these terms. He borrowed them from the terminology of the major debate over military history then under way among scholars and soldiers in Wilhelmine Germany. The inventor of the antithesis between *Ermattungsstrategie* and *Niederwerfungsstrategie* was Hans Delbrück, the most original military historian of his day. Delbrück had first presented his theory of the two types of war in 1881, at an inaugural lecture to the University of Berlin, in which he contrasted the campaigns of Frederick II and Napoleon—the first as an exemplar of the protracted strategy of attrition characteristic of the European ancien régimes, the second as the prototype of the rapid strategy of overthrow inaugurated by the mass popular armies of the modern epoch.[10] Vehemently contested within Prussian

---

10 Hans Delbrück, *Über den Kampf Napoleons mit dem alten Europa*, later expanded into *Über die Verschiedenheit der Strategie Friedrichs und Napoleons*, Berlin 1881. The remote inspiration for Delbrück's theory was

academic circles, for whom Delbrück's account of the Frederician wars verged on contumely, the theory of the two strategies was developed by Delbrück in a series of writings which culminated in his monumental *Geschichte der Kriegskunst im Rahmen der politischen Geschichte*, spanning the evolution of military theory and practice from antiquity to the twentieth century.[11] Successive volumes of this work were keenly studied in the ranks of the German High Command and those of German Social Democracy alike. Schlieffen, Chief of the General Staff, plotted his war exercises meticulously against Delbrück's categories (opting eventually for a strategy of overthrow, not of attrition, in his plan against France). Mehring, in *Die Neue Zeit*, enthusiastically recommended Delbrück's histories to working class readers in 1908 as 'the most significant work produced by the historical writing of bourgeois Germany in the new century'.[12] In an essay on them over one hundred pages long, Mehring dwelt on the perennial validity of the opposition between attrition and overthrow for the art of war. He ended by remarking pointedly that Delbrück had written a work of 'scientific research in a field in which the modern labour movement has a more than merely scientific interest'.[13]

---

the postscript note in Book 8 of Clausewitz's *Vom Kriege* (from 1827), where Clausewitz discussed the case of wars with a 'limited aim', which therefore departed from his general schema that the aim of war was the 'overthrow' of the enemy. See Clausewitz, *Vom Kriege*, Bonn 1952, pp. 882–906.

11 The first three volumes appeared in 1900, 1901 and 1907 successively. The fourth volume was published after the war, in 1920. For the 'two strategies', see especially Vol. 1, pp. 123–7, and Vol. IV, pp. 333–63. Otto Hintze wrote the most effective criticism of Delbrück's account of Frederick II's military practice.

12 See '*Eine Geschichte der Kriegskunst*', now in Franz Mehring, *Gesammelte Schriften*, Vol. 8, Berlin 1967, devoted to his military writings and entitled *Kriegsgeschichte und Militärfrage*, p. 135.

13 Ibid., pp. 147–50, 200.

It was Kautsky who then took the next step of annexing Delbrück's military concepts—without acknowledgment—into a political debate on the strategic perspectives of proletarian struggle against capitalism. The occasion of his intervention was a fateful one. For it was in order to rebut the demand by Luxemburg for the adoption of militant mass strikes, during the SPD's campaign for a democratisation of the neo-feudal Prussian electoral system, that Kautsky counterposed the necessity of a more prudent 'war of attrition' by the German proletariat against its class enemy, without the risks involved in mass strikes. The introduction of the theory of two strategies—attrition and over-throw—was thus the precipitate of the scission within orthodox German Marxism before the First World War.[14]

The formal similarity of the opposition 'strategy of overthrow-strategy of attrition', and 'war of manoeuvre-war of position' is, of course, striking.[15] However, the substantive analogies between the two pairs of concepts, in the texts of Kautsky and of Gramsci, are even more so. To support his argument for the superiority

14  The polemic between Kautsky and Luxemburg took the form of a sequence of lengthy exchanges in *Die Neue Zeit* in 1910. These were, in order: Kautsky, '*Was nun?*' 8 April, pp. 35–40, 15 April, pp. 65–80; Luxemburg, '*Ermattung oder Kampf?*' 27 May, pp. 257–66, 3 July, pp. 291–305; Kautsky, '*Eine neue Strategie*', 17 June, pp. 364–74, 24 June, pp. 412–21; Luxemburg, '*Die Theorie und die Praxis*', 22 July, pp. 564–78, 29 July, pp. 626–42; Kautsky, '*Zwischen Baden und Luxemburg*', 5 August, pp. 652–67; Luxemburg, '*Zur Richtigstellung*', 19 August, pp. 756–60; Kautsky, '*Schlusswort*', 19 August, pp. 760–65. It should be emphasised that Kautsky nowhere attributed his categories to Delbrück, whom he cited only once in the entire polemic, in a passing reference to ancient history. Luxemburg, consequently, seems to have remained unaware of the source of Kautsky's ideas to the end.

15  Delbrück expressly equated a 'strategy of attrition' (*Ermattungsstrategie*) with a 'war of position' (*Stellungskrieg*), during the First World War. He advocated the latter for the German struggle in the West, by contrast with Schlieffen.

of a strategy of attrition over a strategy of overthrow, Kautsky evoked precisely the same historical and geographical contrasts as Gramsci was to do in his discussion of war of position and war of manoeuvre. The coincidence is arresting. Thus Kautsky too fixed the predominance of a 'strategy of overthrow' (Gramsci: 'war of manoeuvre') from 1789 to 1870, and its supersession by a 'strategy of attrition' (Gramsci: 'war of position') from the fall of the Commune: 'Through a coincidence of propitious circumstances, the revolutionaries in France during the years 1789–93 succeeded in bringing down the dominant regime in a bold attack in a few decisive blows. This strategy of overthrow was then the only one available for a revolutionary class, in an absolutist police state which excluded any possibility of building parties, or of the popular masses exercising any constitutional influence on the government. Any strategy of attrition would have failed because the government, confronted with opponents who wanted to unite for a durable resistance to it, could always cut off their possibilities of organisation or coordination. This strategy of overthrow was still in full bloom when our party was founded in Germany. The success of Garibaldi in Italy and the glittering, if eventually defeated, struggles of the Polish Insurrection immediately preceded Lassalle's agitation and the founding of the International. The Paris Commune followed soon afterwards. But it was precisely the Commune which showed that the days of a tactic of overthrow were now past. It was adapted to political circumstances characterised by a dominant capital city and an inadequate communications system which made it impossible to concentrate large masses of troops quickly from the countryside; and to a level of technique in street-planning and military equipment which gave considerable chances to street-fighting. It was then that the foundations of a new strategy of the revolutionary class were laid, which Engels eventually counterposed so sharply to the old revolutionary strategy in his introduction to *The Class Struggles in France*, and which can very well be designated a strategy of attrition. This strategy has hitherto won us the most shining successes, endowed the proletariat from year to year with greater strength, and put it ever more at the centre of European politics.'[16]

The nub of this strategy of attrition were successive electoral campaigns, which Kautsky hopefully asserted might give the SPD a numerical majority in the Reichstag next year. Denying that aggressive mass strikes had any relevance in the present conjuncture in Germany, Kautsky went on to advance the idea of a geopolitical separation between Eastern and Western Europe. In Tsarist Russia, Kautsky wrote, there was no universal suffrage, no legal rights of assembly, no freedom of the press. In 1905, the government was isolated at home, the army defeated abroad, and the peasantry in revolt across the vast and uncoordinated imperial territory. In these circumstances, a strategy of overthrow was still possible. For the Russian proletariat, which lacked elementary political or economic rights, could launch an 'amorphous and primitive' revolutionary general strike, directed indifferently against government and employers.[17] The gathering storm of mass strikes in Russia then spontaneously escalated to a decisive contest with the state. In the event, the 'policy of violence' pursued by the Russian working class encountered ultimate defeat. But its strategy of overthrow was the natural product of Russian society's historical backwardness.

'The conditions for a strike in Western Europe and especially in Germany', Kautsky went on, 'are, however, very different

---

16 'Was nun?' p. 38. Compare Gramsci's text cited on pp. 39–40 above.
17 'Eine neue Strategie', p. 369.

from those in pre-revolutionary and revolutionary Russia.'[18] In Western Europe, the workers were more numerous and better organised, and they had long possessed civic liberties. They were also confronted with a stronger class enemy, equipped—above all in Germany—with a disciplined army and bureaucracy. The Prussian state machine, in fact, was now the most powerful in Europe. The working class was also more isolated from other classes than in Russia. Hence tumultuous mass strikes such as occurred during 1905 in Russia were inappropriate in the West. 'Demonstrations of this sort have never yet occurred in Western Europe. Nor is it probable that they will do so—not in spite, but because of half a century of the socialist movement, social-democratic organisation and political freedom.'[19] In these circumstances, to unleash mass strikes to secure the reform of the Prussian franchise, as Luxemburg demanded, would merely compromise the chances of the SPD at the next Reichstag elections. Formally, Kautsky did not deny that in 'the final battle' of the class struggle, a transition to a strategy of overthrow would be necessary in the West too. But the weapon of the mass strike should be reserved solely for this decisive engagement, when victory or defeat would be absolute. For the moment, 'preliminary skirmishes should not be fought with heavy artillery'.[20] The only correct path in the West was a strategy of attrition, recalling that of Fabius Cunctator in Ancient Rome.[21]

Luxemburg, whom Gramsci reproached for her 'mysticism'

---

18  Ibid.
19  Ibid., p. 370.
20  Ibid., p. 374.
21  'Was Nun?' pp. 37–8. Kautsky, of course, knew of the existence of the Fabian Society, but appears to have forgotten the revealing coincidence of eponymous hero.

in his central text on East and West,[22] grasped the logic of
Kautsky's contrast between the two zones immediately. The
polemic between them on just this issue was the occasion for
her political break with Kautsky, four years in advance of Lenin,
who only understood it when war arrived in 1914. Luxemburg
denounced the 'whole theory of the two strategies' and its 'crude
contrast between revolutionary Russia and parliamentary
Western Europe',[23] as a rationalisation of Kautsky's refusal of
mass strikes and his capitulation to electoralism. She rejected
Kautsky's description of the Russian Revolution of 1905: 'The
picture of a chaotic, "amorphous and primitive" strike of the
Russian workers … is a flowering fantasy.'[24] It was not political
backwardness but advance that distinguished the Russian proletariat within the European working class. 'The Russian strikes
and mass strikes, which gave form to so audacious a creation
as the famous Petersburg Soviet of Workers' Delegates for the
unitary leadership of the whole movement in the enormous
Empire, were so little "amorphous and primitive" that in daring,
strength, solidarity, persistence, material achievements, progressive goals and organisational successes, they can calmly be set
by the side of any "West European" trade-union movement.'[25]

Luxemburg dismissed Kautsky's circumspect assessment
of the Prussian State, retorting that he had confused its police
crudity and brutality with political strength, for the purposes of
justifying timidity towards it. Kautsky's avowed retention of the
use of a mass strike for the single apocalyptic contingency of a
'final battle' in the distant future was a token clause, designed to

---

22  QC III, pp. 1613–14; SPN, p. 233.
23  'Die Theorie und die Praxis', p. 576.
24  Ibid., p. 572.
25  Ibid.

absolve the SPD from any commitment to serious struggles in the concrete present, allowing it to settle for the most mundane opportunism. Luxemburg's political instinct led her to isolate the ultimate drift of Kautsky's arguments unerringly: 'In practice, Comrade Kautsky directs us insistently towards the coming Reichstag elections. These are the basic pillars of his strategy of attrition. It is from the Reichstag elections that salvation is to be expected. They will surely bring us an overwhelming victory, they will create a wholly new situation, they will immediately "put in our pocket the key to this tremendous historical situation". In a word, there are so many violins in the heaven of the next Reichstag elections that we would be criminally light-minded to think of any mass strike when we have before us such a certain victory, put "in our pocket" by the voting slip.'[26]

Luxemburg's own position in these debates was not without its flaws. She made no adequate reply to Kautsky's characterisation of the Russian state, as opposed to the Russian working class, evading the genuine problem of its structural difference from the Western states of the time, which Kautsky had not been wrong to emphasise. Nor did she possess, here or elsewhere, any etched theory of the conquest of power by the proletariat—her conception of mass strikes as continuous exercises in working class autonomy and combativity blurring the inevitably discontinuous rupture of a revolutionary rising against the capitalist state itself, necessarily transcending the level of a strike.[27] However, these limitations were secondary when compared with the acuity of her insight into the dynamics of Kautsky's theory. Her prescience

---

26 'Ermattung oder Kampf?' pp. 294–5.
27 Luxemburg, of course, always asserted the need for proletarian insurrection to achieve socialism: but she tended to merge it into vaster ongoing waves of working class militancy, in which its incommensurability was obscured.

about its evolution is all the more impressive when it is compared with Lenin's complaisance towards Kautsky.

For the debate within German social democracy had a revealing sequel within Russian social democracy. A few weeks later, Martov wrote an article in *Die Neue Zeit* on 'The Prussian Debate and Russian Experience'.[28] Warmly approving Kautsky's overall theses, Martov argued that Russia was actually in no way exempt from their lessons. Luxemburg should not be allowed to utilise the Russian Revolution of 1905 as her 'trump card' against official SPD policy in Germany, nor her account of it be conceded by Western socialists, in the name of the *privilegium odiosum* of Russian exceptionalism. Russian experience was now similar in every way to European experience as a whole. Where it had diverged in 1905, it had ended in disaster. The blending of economic with political strikes, vaunted by Luxemburg, was a weakness rather than a strength of the Russian proletariat. The Moscow uprising was the calamitous result of an 'artificial' propulsion of the movement towards a 'decisive clash' with the state. For Kautsky's sagacity was then unknown in Russia: 'The idea of a "strategy of attrition" occurred to no-one.' Now, however, after the failure of the extremism of 1905, it was the responsibility of the Russian labour movement to adopt it. 'The proletariat must strive, not merely to struggle, but to win.'[29]

Martov's prompt utilisation of Kautsky's theses to justify Menshevik policies in Russia duly provoked a reply from the Polish Bolshevik Marchlewski in *Die Neue Zeit*. Marchlewski's response appears to have pre-empted Lenin's own reply—the latter desisting from a draft after Kautsky had accepted a prior

---

28   L. Martov, '*Die preussische Diskussion und die russische Erfahrung*', *Die Neue Zeit*, 16 September 1910, pp. 907–19.
29   Ibid., pp. 907, 913, 919.

article on the same subject from the former. Lenin, however, wrote to Marchlewski with suggestions for inclusion in his answer to Martov, most of which were integrated into the published text. The two documents are of the greatest interest. For the burden of Marchlewski's argument was that the Bolsheviks in Russia had—contrary to Martov's distortions—never deviated from the logic of Kautsky's precepts. On the contrary, Marchlewski wrote, 'Lenin's recommendations were—if you like—the same as Kautsky's: due application of a "strategy of overthrow" and of a "strategy of attrition" at the appropriate times for them.'[30] Now, in the long Tsarist reaction after the revolution of 1905, it was the time for a strategy of attrition. Russian social democracy must at present 'learn to speak German'.

Lenin himself meanwhile, in his letter to Marchlewski, endorsed the validity of Kautsky's claims of final intransigence in his polemic with Luxemburg—indeed emphatically reiterated them, despite the alacrity of Martov's appropriation of Kautsky's arguments for a vindication of Menshevism in Russia. 'Rosa Luxemburg argued with Kautsky as to whether in Germany the moment had arrived for *Niederwerfungsstrategie*, and Kautsky plainly and bluntly stated that he considered this moment was unavoidable and imminent but had not yet arrived … All the Mensheviks seized on Rosa Luxemburg's dispute with Kautsky in order to declare Kautsky a "Menshevik". Martov is trying his hardest, by means of petty and miserable diplomacy, to deepen the gulf between Rosa Luxemburg and Karl Kautsky. These wretched devices cannot succeed. Revolutionary social-democrats may argue about the timing of

---

30 J. Karsky (Marchlewski), '*Ein Missverstandnis*', *Die Neue Zeit*, 28 October 1910, p. 102.

*Niederwerfungsstrategie* in Germany, but not about its appro-
priateness in Russia in 1905.'[31]

The contrast with Luxemburg is striking. For Luxemburg
perceived at once that the real effect of Kautsky's arguments was
a sophisticated apology for reformism. Her vigorous denuncia-
tions of them received their vindication by the end of the polemic
between the two. For Luxemburg's characterisation of Kautsky's
theory as what she called *Nichtsalsparlimentarismus*—nothing
but parliamentarism—was finally confirmed in so many words
by Kautsky himself in one of his closing rejoinders, in a formulation which sums up his position in a classic expression of what
can be called the social-democratic 'defence clause': 'The more
democratic the constitution of a country, the less there exist conditions for a mass strike, the less necessary for the masses does
such a strike become, and therefore the less often it happens.
Where the proletariat possesses sufficient electoral rights, a
mass strike is only to be expected as a defensive measure—as a
means to protect voting rights or a parliament with strong social-
democratic representation, against a government that refuses to
obey the will of the people's representatives.'[32]

Gramsci, cut off from the outside world in prison during the
thirties, was unaware of these precedents while he struggled to

31   Lenin, *Collected Works*, Vol. 34, pp. 427–8. Martov, in Lenin's angry phrase,
     was '"deepening" (botching) Kautsky', by denying the applicability of a *Nie-
     derwerfungsstrategie* to the year 1905 in Russia (p. 427). Actually, Kautsky's
     comments on what he termed the 'policy of violence' of the Russian
     proletariat in 1905–6 had evinced a thinly disguised lack of enthusiasm.
     Martov's reading of them was thus not far from the mark.

32   '*Zwischen Baden und Luxemburg*', p. 665. There is no space here to go into
     the history of the 'defence clause'—now standard in the official documents
     of the heirs of the Third International. Suffice it to say that it was a common
     patrimony of the classical parties of the Second International. Bebel, Turati
     and Bauer all devoted major speeches to it, at respective party congresses
     of the SPD, PSI and OSPD.

forge concepts to resist the renewal of adventurism within the Comintern. It was in this context that he was able to produce a notion formally analogous to that of Kautsky (strategy of attrition/war of position), without seeing its dangers. Gramsci's 'war of position' was intended, as we have seen, as a reply to Thalheimer's and Lukács's 'war of manoeuvre'—in the spirit, he believed, of the Comintern Congress that had condemned them. The errors of the theory of the *Teilaktion* have already been discussed. Did Gramsci's formula, however, completely correct them? It will be noticed that what he did was in effect to invert their way of posing the problem. Revolutionary strategy in Gramsci's account becomes a long, immobile trench war between two camps in fixed positions, in which each tries to undermine the other culturally and politically. 'The siege is a reciprocal one', Gramsci wrote, 'concentrated, difficult, demanding exceptional qualities of patience and invention.'[33] There is no doubt that the danger of adventurism disappears in this perspective, with its overwhelming emphasis on the ideological allegiance of the masses as the central object of struggle, to be gained only by pursuit of a united front within the working class. But what happens to the phase of insurrection itself—the storming and destruction of the state machine that for Marx or Lenin were inseparable from the proletarian revolution? Gramsci never relinquished the basic tenets of classical Marxism on the ultimate need for a violent seizure of state power, but his strategic formula for the West failed to integrate them. The mere counterposition of 'war of position' to 'war of manoeuvre' in any Marxist strategy in the end becomes an opposition between reformism and adventurism.

33   *QC* II, p. 802; *SPN*, p. 239.

An objection must immediately occur to such a judgement. Why should Gramsci not have intended the strategy of 'war of position' to be a preparation for a concluding 'war of manoeuvre' against the class enemy? In other words, did he not in fact advocate a thesis that Lenin had wrongly ascribed to Kautsky—the necessity of 'a transition from the "strategy of attrition" to the "strategy of overthrow"', a transition which was 'inevitable' in the period of a political crisis when 'the revolution reaches its highest intensity'?[34] In this schema, Gramsci's war of position would correspond to the phase in which a revolutionary party seeks to win the masses ideologically (consensually) to the cause of socialism, prior to the phase in which it will lead them politically into a final (coercive) revolt against the bourgeois State. 'Hegemony' would then indeed be exercised within civil society, in the formation of a class bloc of the exploited, while 'dictatorship' would be asserted over against the exploiters, in the forcible destruction of the state apparatus that secured their rule.

Such an interpretation would conform to the classical principles of historical materialism. Yet in all the 2,000 pages of the *Prison Notebooks*, there is only one, glancing sentence that appears to be in concordance with it. Even that is oblique and ambiguous. At the very end of the long passage comparing East and West which we have cited so often, Gramsci penned a short afterthought—gratuitously suppressed by his editors after the war. 'One attempt to start a revision of the current tactical methods was perhaps that outlined by Trotsky at the Fourth World Congress, when he made a comparison between

---

34   Lenin, *Collected Works*, Vol. 16, p. 383. This article contains the formal reply that Lenin drafted for publication in *Die Neue Zeit*, in answer to Martov's use of Kautsky's 'strategy of attrition', during the composition of which he wrote his letter to Marchlewski. The article was refused by Kautsky and never printed in Germany.

the Eastern and Western fronts. The former had fallen at once, but unprecedented struggles had then ensued; in the case of the latter, the struggles would occur beforehand. The question, therefore, was whether civil society resists before or after the attempt to seize power; where the latter occurs, and so on. However, the question was outlined only in a brilliant, literary form, without directives of a practical character.'[35]

In this passage alone can be found a fleeting instance of the correct theoretical and temporal order in which Gramsci's concepts should have been deployed, to yield a revolutionary political strategy for advanced capitalism. For in the West, the resistance of 'civil society' would precisely have to be overcome before that of the state, by the work of the United Front—yet victory within this arena would then have to be succeeded by what Gramsci here directly calls an armed 'assault' (*assalto*) on the state. Unfortunately, the insight contained in this allusion to another thinker was a passing one. The weight of Gramsci's own imagery—indeed cast in a 'brilliant, literary form'—in his central strategic texts goes in the opposite direction. There it is the state which is merely an 'outer ditch', and civil society which is the 'powerful system of fortresses and earthworks' that lies 'behind' it. In other words, it is the civil society of capitalism—repeatedly described as the domain of consent—that becomes the ultimate barrier to the victory of the socialist movement. The war of position is then the struggle by the organised working class to win hegemony over it—a hegemony which by tacit definition merges into a political paramountcy over the social formation as a whole.

---

35   *QC* III, p. 1616; *SPN*, p. 236. To Quintin Hoare belongs the credit of having first seen the significance of this passage, in his editing of the political sections of *Selections from the Prison Notebooks*. Gramsci was referring to Trotsky's speech to the Fourth World Congress of the Comintern in 1922.

'In politics, war of position is hegemony', Gramsci wrote, while 'hegemony is rule by permanently organised consent'.[36]

The theoretical slippage noted earlier thus recurs again in Gramsci's strategic thought, with yet more serious consequences. For in a direct reversal of Lenin's order of battle, Gramsci expressly relegated 'war of movement' to a merely preliminary or subsidiary role in the West, and promoted 'war of position' to the concluding and decisive role in the struggle between labour and capital. In so doing, he was finally trapped by the logic of his own concepts. The fatal passage reads: 'The war of position demands enormous sacrifices by infinite masses of people. So an unprecedented concentration of hegemony is necessary, and hence a more "interventionist" government, which will take the offensive more directly against oppositionists and organise permanently the "impossibility" of internal disintegration—with controls of every kind, political, administrative and other, rein-forcement of the hegemonic "positions" of the dominant group, and so on. All this indicates that we have entered a culminating phase in the political-historical situation, since in politics the "war of position", once won, is decisive definitively. In politics, in other words, the war of manoeuvre subsists so long as it is a question of winning positions that are not decisive.'[37]

---

36  *QC* II, p. 973. *QC* III, p. 1636; *SPN*, p. 80n.

37  *QC* II, p. 802; *SPN*, p. 239. It has sometimes been thought that this passage refers to the fascist, rather than to the communist, movement. A careful study of it seems to exclude this hypothesis. The 'enormous sacrifices' made by the 'masses' are unmistakably a reference to the working class. Similarly, Gramsci would never have regarded fascism as definitively victorious in Italy—which its installation in power, in the context of this paragraph, would have made it. In general, the emphasis on ultra-centralised authority and discipline here should probably be linked to the (otherwise enigmatic) call for the 'sole command' of a proletarian Foch in the major text on East and West: *QC* II, p. 866; *SPN*, p. 238.

The errors of this text have their suspect symptom: the disquieting claims for the necessity of a more authoritarian command within the ranks of the working class, capable of suppressing all dissent. The association of the strategy of a war of position with a centralised uniformity of political expression, in homage to the worst side of the Comintern, is not a reassuring one. In fact, the socialist revolution will only triumph in the West by a maximum expansion—not constriction—of proletarian democracy: for its experience alone, in parties or councils, can enable the working class to learn the real limits of bourgeois democracy, and equip it historically to surpass them. For a Marxist strategy within advanced capitalism to settle on a war of position and an ethos of command to achieve the final emancipation of labour is to ensure its own defeat. When the hour of reckoning in the class struggle arrives, proletarian liberty and insurgency go together. It is their combination, and no other, that can constitute a true social war of movement capable of overthrowing capital in its strongest bastions.

The political solution for the future of the Western working class that Gramsci sought in prison, in the end eluded him. The perspective of a war of position was a deadlock. In the final analysis, the function of this idea in Gramsci's thought seems to have been that of a kind of moral metaphor: it represented a sense of stoical adjustment to the loss of any immediate hope of victory in the West. In one of those coincidences that are a signature of the time, the Marxist thinker in Western Europe whose fate was closest to that of Gramsci in the thirties reproduced the same idea in his very different work. Walter Benjamin, fellow victim of fascism, expressed his political pessimism in the motto of a 'tactic of attrition' (*Ermattungstaktik*)—for which his friend Brecht commemorated him, unaware of any anterior history, on his death.[38] The poetic register of Benjamin's notion tells us something about the scientific status of Gramsci's formula. The debt that every contemporary Marxist owes to Gramsci can only be properly acquitted if his writings are taken with the seriousness of real criticism. In the labyrinth of the notebooks, Gramsci lost his way. Against his own intention, formal conclusions can be drawn from his work that lead away from revolutionary socialism.

Is it necessary to add that Gramsci was himself proof against any sort of reformism? The parliamentarist conclusions of Kautsky's strategic theory were absolutely foreign to him: his work is strewn elsewhere with assertions of the imperative need for a revolutionary overthrow of the capitalist state. We do not even have to look back at his countless statements before prison and censorship. In the document that can be regarded as Gramsci's effective political testament, his final direct counsel to the militants of the Italian working class recorded by Athos Lisa, in which he insisted in defiance of Third Period doctrines on the necessity for popular intermediary objectives in the struggle against fascism—above all, a constituent assembly—he also left no doubt about his commitment to ultimate objectives, as Marx and Lenin would have thought of them: 'The violent conquest of power necessitates the creation by the party of the working class of an organisation of a military type, pervasively implanted in every branch of the bourgeois State apparatus, and capable

---

38 *'Ermattungstaktik war's, was dir behagte'* ('Tactics of attrition are what you enjoyed'): 'An Walter Benjamin', in Bertolt Brecht, *Gesammelte Werke*, Vol. X, Frankfurt 1967, p. 828. Brecht had few illusions in the practical efficacy of his friend's perspective: *'Der Feind, der dich von deinem Büchern jagte / Lässt sich von unsereinem nicht ermatten'* ('The enemy who drives you from your books / Will not be worn away by the likes of us').

of wounding and inflicting heavy blows on it at the decisive moment of struggle.'[39]

Gramsci not merely asserted the need for proletarian revolution in classical terms; many have done that verbally since. He fought and suffered a long agony for it. Not merely his work, but his life is incomprehensible without this vocation. Gramsci himself was only too well aware of the conditions of his struggle against illness, isolation and death. The central passages in his notebooks on the distinction between East and West are all cast in the form of an extended military analogy: 'artillery', 'trenches', 'commanders', 'manoeuvre', 'position'. The same man laconically warns us against any easy reading of his own vocabulary. 'In saying all this, the general criterion should be remembered that comparisons between military art and politics should always be taken with a pinch of salt—in other words as aids to thought or terms in a *reductio ad absurdum*.'[40]

The conditions of Gramsci's composition in prison produced a non-unitary, fragmentary theory, which inherently allowed discrepancies and incoherences in it. Nothing reveals this more clearly than the references to Trotsky in the central texts discussed in this study. For in them, the concept of 'Permanent Revolution' is repeatedly the formal object of Gramsci's criticism, as the alleged expression of a 'war of manoeuvre'. Yet it was Trotsky who led the attack with Lenin on the generalised theory of the 'revolutionary offensive' at the Third Congress of the Comintern. It was Trotsky, again with Lenin, who was the main architect of the United Front which Gramsci equated

---

39  For the text of the *Athos Lisa Report*, see pp. 156–68 below. In it, Gramsci discusses the military problems of a future Italian revolution with a notable technical and organisational precision.

40  *QC* I, p. 120; *SPN*, p. 231.

with his 'war of position'. Finally, it was Trotsky, not Lenin, who wrote the document that was the classical theorisation of the United Front in the twenties.[41] Gramsci's confusion was here virtually total. The political proof of it was to be very concrete. For during the height of the Third Period in 1932, Gramsci in the prison of Turi di Bari and Trotsky on the island of Prinkipo developed effectively identical positions on the political situation in Italy, in diametric contrast to the official line of the PCI and of the Comintern. Prisoner and exile alike called for a United Front of working class resistance to fascism including the social-democratic parties, and a transitional perspective including the possibility of a restoration of bourgeois democracy in Italy after the fall of fascism.[42] Neither, of course, was aware of the other, in this convergence in the political night of the time.

There is a further irony in Gramsci's confusion, beyond even this. For in point of fact, it was above all Trotsky who provided the working class movement, East or West, with a scientific critique of both the ideas of 'war of manoeuvre' and 'war of position', in the field where they really obtained—military strategy proper. For the political doctrines that emerged within the revolutionary movement of Central Europe in 1920–21 had their military equivalent in Russia. There, Frunze and Tukhachevsky played the role of Lukács and Thalheimer. In the great military debates in the USSR after the Civil War, Frunze, Tukhachevsky, Gusev and others had argued that the essence of revolutionary warfare was

41  'On the United Front', in *The First Five Years of the Communist International*, Vol. II, New York, 1953, pp. 91–104.

42  For Gramsci's views, see Paolo Spriano, *Storia del Partito Communista Italiano*, Vol. II, Turin 1969, pp. 262–74. Trotsky's analyses of the Italian situation are to be found in *Writings of Leon Trotsky 1929* and *1930*, New York 1975; and *1930–1931*, New York 1973. They are collected and discussed in Silvio Corvisieri, *Trotskij e il Communismo Italiano*, Rome 1969, pp. 326–35.

permanent attack, or war of manoeuvre. Tukhachevsky declared: 'Strategic reserves, the utility of which was always doubtful, we need not at all in our war. Now there is only one question: how to use numbers to gain the maximum force of the blow. There is one answer: release all troops in the attack, not holding in reserve a single bayonet.'[43] Frunze claimed that the lessons of the Civil War demonstrated that the primacy of the offensive for a revolutionary strategy coincided with the social nature of the proletariat itself: 'The tactics of the Red Army were and will be inspired with activity in the spirit of bold and energetically conducted offensive operations. This proceeds from the class nature of the workers' and peasants' army and at the same time coincides with the exigencies of military art.'[44] War of position, characteristic of the First World War and of the bourgeoisie, was henceforward an anachronism. 'Manoeuvre is the sole means of securing victory', wrote Tukhachevsky.[45]

Trotsky, as we have seen, fought against the 'theory of the offensive' as a strategy within the Comintern. He now conducted a companion battle against it as a military doctrine within the Red Army. Replying to Frunze and others, Trotsky made the comparison himself: 'Unfortunately, there are not a few simpletons of the offensive among our new fashioned doctrinaires who, under the banner of a military theory, are seeking to introduce into our military circulation the same unilateral "leftist" tendencies which at the Third World Congress of the Comintern attained their fruition in the guise of the theory of the offensive: inasmuch (!) as we are living in a revolutionary epoch, therefore(!) the Communist Party must implement

---

43  *Voina Klassov*, Moscow 1921, p. 55.
44  Theses submitted to the Eleventh Party Congress of the CPSU.
45  *Voina Klassov*, p. 105.

the policy of the offensive. To translate "leftism" into the language of military doctrine is to multiply this error many times over.[46]

Combating these conceptions, Trotsky exposed the fallacy of generalizing from the experience of the Civil War, in which both sides (not just the Red Army) had primarily used manoeuvre, because of the backwardness of the social organisation and military technique of the country. 'Let me point out that we are not the inventors of the manoeuvrist principle. Our enemies also made extensive use of it, owing to the fact that relatively small numbers of troops were deployed over enormous distances and because of wretched means of communication.'[47] But above all Trotsky repeatedly criticised any strategic theory that fetishised either manoeuvre or position into an immutable or absolute principle. All wars would combine position and manoeuvre, and any strategy that unilaterally excluded one or the other was suicidal. 'It is possible to state with certainty that even in our super-manoeuvrist strategy during the Civil War the element of positionalism did exist and in certain instances played an important role.'[48] Therefore, Trotsky concluded: 'Defense and offense enter as variable moments into combat ... Without the offensive, victory cannot be gained. But victory is gained by him who attacks when it is necessary to attack and not by him who attacks first.'[49] In other words, position and manoeuvre had a necessarily complementary relationship in any military strategy. To dismiss either one or the other was to invite defeat and capitulation.

---

46  *Military Writings*, New York 1969, p. 47.
47  Ibid., p. 25.
48  Ibid., p. 85.
49  Ibid., pp. 65, 88.

Having disposed of false analogies or extrapolations whether in the Red Army or in the Comintern, Trotsky then went on to make the prediction that in a genuinely military conflict between classes—in other words an actual, not a metaphorical, civil war— there would in all probability be a greater positionalism in the West than there had been in the East. All internal wars were naturally more manoeuvrist, because of the scission they effected within state and nation, compared with external wars between nations. In this respect, 'manoeuvrability is not peculiar to a revolutionary army but to civil war as such.'[50] However, the greater historical complexity of economic and social structures in the advanced West would render future civil wars there more positional in character than in Russia. 'In the highly developed countries with their huge living centres, with their White Guard cadres prepared in advance, civil war may assume—and in many cases undoubtedly will assume—a far less mobile, a far more compact character, that is, one approximating to positional war.'[51] In the final, dwindling moments of Gramsci's life, Europe was visited by just such a conflict. The Spanish Civil War was to vindicate Trotsky's judgement arrestingly. Fought on the Manzanares and the Ebro, the battle for the Republic proved a long positional ordeal—lost in the end because the working class could never regain the initiative of manoeuvre essential to victory. If Trotsky's analysis was to be confirmed in Spain, it was because of its pertinence to its object. It was a technical, not a metaphorical, theory of war.

---

50  Ibid., p. 54.

51  Ibid., pp. 84–5. Trotsky was careful to go on immediately to say that this did not mean that military struggle between classes in the West could ever be described as a sheer 'war of position'. For 'Generally speaking, there cannot even be talk of some sort of absolute positionalism, all the more so in a civil war. In question here is the reciprocal relation between the elements of manoeuvrability and positionalism': p. 85.

Trotsky's military accuracy, the product of his experience in the Russian Civil War, did not necessarily confer an equivalent privilege on his political strategy. His knowledge of Germany, England and France was in point of fact greater than that of Gramsci. His writings on the three major social formations of Western Europe in the inter-war period are commensurately superior to those in the *Prison Notebooks*. They contain indeed the only developed theory of a modern capitalist state in classical Marxism, in his texts on Nazi Germany. Yet while Trotsky's historical command of the specific sociopolitical structures of capitalism in the central countries of Western Europe had no equal in his own time, he never posed the problem of a differential strategy for making the socialist revolution in them, unscheduled by that in Russia, with the same anxiety or lucidity as Gramsci. In this essential respect, his questions were less troubled.

# 5

# IMPLICATIONS

Gramsci's answers to his problems did not, as we have seen, resolve them. The lessons of the debate between Kautsky and Luxemburg, the contrast between Lukács and Gramsci, can however today at least yield two simple and concrete propositions. To formulate proletarian strategy in metropolitan capitalism essentially as a war of manoeuvre is to forget the unity and efficacy of the bourgeois state and to pit the working class against it in a series of lethal adventures. To formulate proletarian strategy as essentially a war of position is to forget the necessarily sudden and volcanic character of revolutionary situations, which by the nature of these social formations can never be stabilised for long and therefore need speed and mobility of attack if the opportunity to conquer power is not to be missed. Insurrection, Marx and Engels always emphasised, depends on the art of audacity.

In Gramsci's case, the inadequacies of the formula of a 'war of position' had a clear relationship to the ambiguities of his analysis of bourgeois class power. Gramsci equated 'war of position' with 'civil hegemony', it will be remembered. Thus just as his use of hegemony often tended to imply that the structure of capitalist power in the West essentially rested on culture and consent, so the idea of a war of position tended to imply that the revolutionary work of a Marxist party was essentially that of ideological conversion of the working class—hence its identification with the United Front, whose aim was to win a majority of the Western proletariat to the Third International. In both cases, the role of coercion—repression by the bourgeois state, insurrection by the working class—tends to drop out. The weakness of Gramsci's strategy is symmetrical with that of his sociology.

What is the contemporary relevance of these past debates over Marxist strategy? Any real discussion of the problems of the present would involve many questions to which there has been no allusion here. The limits of a philological survey have dictated these inevitable restrictions. Such central issues as the interconnexion of economic and political struggles in the labour movement, the alliances of the working class in largely post-peasant societies, the contemporary nature of capitalist crises, the possible catalysts and forms of dual power, the development of more advanced institutions of proletarian democracy—wider and freer than any past precedents—are all omitted here. Yet to deliberate in isolation from them on the structures of the bourgeois state and the strategies necessary for the working class to overthrow it, can lead to an irresponsible abstraction—unless these necessary other elements of any Marxist theory of the socialist revolution in the West are always recollected. If we accept this limitation, what can be concluded from the heritage reconstructed in this essay? There is space, and occasion, here for only two comments, confined to the subjects of its debate.

The logic of Marxist theory indicates that it is in the nature of the bourgeois state that, in any final contest, the armed apparatus of repression will displace the ideological apparatuses of parliamentary representation, to re-occupy the dominant position in the structure of capitalist class power. This coercive state machine is the ultimate barrier to a workers' revolution, and can only be broken by pre-emptive counter-coercion. In the nineteenth century, barricades provided the traditional symbol of the latter. Yet Lenin long ago pointed out that these fortifications often had a moral rather than military function: their purpose was classically as much a fraternisation with soldiers as a weapon against them. For in any revolution, the task of a proletarian vanguard, in Lenin's words, is not merely to fight against the troops but for the troops. This does not mean, he emphasised, mere verbal persuasion to join the camp of the proletariat, but a 'physical struggle' by the masses to win them over to the side of the revolution.[1]

An insurrection can only succeed if the repressive apparatus of the state itself divides or disintegrates—as it did in Russia, China or Cuba. The consensual 'convention' that holds the forces of coercion together must, in other words, be breached. The armies of Western Europe, North America and Japan today are composed of conscripts or recruits from the exploited classes, who possess a potential capacity to paralyse counter-revolutionary mobilisation in a general crisis. A key objective of political struggle is thus always to act on the enlisted men with class audacity and resolve, to break the unity of the repressive apparatus of the

---

1   'Of course, unless the revolution assumes a mass character and affects the troops, there can be no question of serious struggle. That we must work among the troops goes without saying. But we must not imagine that they will come over to our side at one stroke, as a result of persuasion or their own convictions. The Moscow uprising clearly demonstrated how stereotyped and lifeless this view is. As a matter of fact, the wavering of the troops which is inevitable in every truly popular movement, leads to a real fight for the troops whenever the revolutionary struggle becomes acute.' Lenin, *Collected Works*, Vol. 11, p. 174.

state. In other words, a proletarian rising is always a political operation, whose fundamental aim is not to inflict casualties on the enemy, but to rally all the exploited masses together, whether in overalls or in uniform, women as well as men, for the creation of a new popular power. Yet it is also, however, necessarily a military operation. For no matter how successful the working class is in dividing the coercive apparatus of the state (army or police), detaching major segments from it, and winning them over to the cause of the revolution, there still always remains an irreducible core of counter-revolutionary forces, specially trained and hardened in their repressive functions, who cannot be converted; who can only be defeated. The Petrograd Garrison went over to the Military Revolutionary Committee: the Junkers and the Cossacks in the Winter Palace still resisted. The infantry and artillery may have rallied to the cause of socialism in Portugal: the commandos and air force remained intact to suppress it.

Where the domestic institutions of repression disintegrate too suddenly or drastically, it is the external intervention of stronger military apparatuses from abroad, controlled by more powerful bourgeois states, that will be deployed—the 'foreign currency' of coercion towards which local capital moves in flight when its own reserves sink too low. The examples, from Russia to Spain, from Cuba to Vietnam, are common knowledge. The duality—internal or international—of the armed apparatus of the enemy is an unvarying element of every revolution. Trotsky captured it with accuracy: 'The workers must in advance take all measures to draw the soldiers to the side of the people by means of preliminary agitation; but at the same time they must foresee that the government will always be left with a sufficient number of dependable or semi-dependable soldiers for them to call out for the purposes of quelling an insurrection; and consequently in the final resort the question has to be decided by an armed conflict.'[2] The determination of the capitalist state in the final instance by coercion thus holds true of the coercive apparatus itself. Ideological and political struggle can undermine a bourgeois military machine in a revolutionary crisis, by a consensual conquest of the men enlisted in it. But the hard core of professional counter-revolutionary units—marines, paratroops, riot police or paramilitary gendarmerie—can only be swept away by the coercive attack of the masses. From beginning to end, the laws of the capitalist state are reflected and refused in the rules of a socialist revolution.

Such a revolution will only occur in the West when the masses have made the experience of a proletarian democracy that is tangibly superior to bourgeois democracy. The sole way for the victory of socialism to be secured in these societies is for it to represent incontestably more, not less, freedom for the vast majority of the population. It is the untapped store of popular energies any inception of a real workers' democracy would release that will provide the explosive force capable of ending the rule of capital. For the exhibition of a new, unprivileged liberty must start before the old order is structurally cancelled by the conquest of the state. The name of this necessary overlap is dual power. The ways and means of its emergence—with or without the presence of a workers' government in office—constitute the critical intermediate problem of any socialist revolution. For the moment, however, the working class movement in most of the countries of the West is some distance away from this threshold. It is no doubt the case that the majority of the exploited population in every major capitalist social formation today remains

2   *Where Is Britain Going?*, London 1973, p. 87.

subject in one way or another to reformist or capitalist ideology. It is here that the most durable political theme of Gramsci's *Notebooks* acquires its sense. For the task that the United Front was designed to acquit is still unsolved fifty years later. The masses in North America, Western Europe and Japan have yet to be won over to revolutionary socialism. Therefore, the central problematic of the United Front—the final strategic advice of Lenin to the Western working class movement before his death, the first concern of Gramsci in prison—retains all its validity today. It has never been historically surpassed. The imperative need remains to win the working class before there can be any talk of winning power. The means of achieving this conquest— not of the institutions of the state, but of the convictions of workers, although in the end there will be no separation of the two—are the prime agenda of any real socialist strategy today.

The international disputes which united and divided Luxemburg, Lenin, Lukács, Gramsci, Bordiga or Trotsky on these issues represent the last great strategic debate in the European workers' movement. Since then, there has been little significant theoretical development of the political problems of revolutionary strategy in metropolitan capitalism that has had any direct contact with the masses. The structural divorce between original Marxist theory and the main organisations of the working class in Europe has yet to be historically resolved. The May–June revolt in France, the upheaval in Portugal, the approaching denouement in Spain, presage the end of this long divorce, but have not accomplished it. The classical debates, therefore, still remain in many respects the most advanced limit of reference we possess today. It is thus not mere archaism to recall the strategic confrontations which occurred four or five decades ago. To reappropriate them, on the contrary, is a step towards a

Marxist discussion that has the—necessarily modest—hope of assuming an 'initial shape' of correct theory today. Régis Debray has spoken, in a famous paragraph, of the constant difficulty of being contemporary with our present. In Europe at least, we have yet to be sufficiently contemporary with our past.

# ANNEXE: ATHOS LISA'S REPORT

## Introductory Note

In the autumn of 1930, Gramsci gave a series of talks in the courtyard of the jail at Turi near Bari where he was held, in which he expressed his political ideas directly to his fellow prisoners without having to resort to the prudent ciphers and allusions of his notebooks, composed under the eye of censors. That we have a record of what he said is due to one of his listeners, who at the time strongly disagreed with him. Athos Lisa, an almost exact contemporary—he was born in 1890, Gramsci a few months later—was a railway worker from Pisa. Originally a socialist, after escaping from the police to France he joined the Communist Party in 1924, returning to Italy and working in its underground until his arrest in late 1926. Sentenced to nine years in prison, after spending two of these in the harshest confinement on the islands of Santo Stefano and Pianosa, he was transferred to Turi a few weeks after Gramsci started giving his lectures, remaining there till the autumn of 1931, when he was invalided out to another prison in Lazio, returning to Turi a year later. In October 1932 he was included in an amnesty, and on his release made his way to Paris, where the exiled leadership of the PCI was based.

There in February 1933 he wrote a report for it on the imprisoned Gramsci's political views, for which Togliatti thanked him and told him never to speak of it to anyone. In France he served in Red Aid, the Communist organisation for support of political prisoners, and did relief work for victims of the Spanish Civil War, before joining the Resistance in the Alpes Maritimes during the Second World War. After Liberation he helped the CGT produce a paper for Italian workers in France. At the height of the Cold War, he was expelled from France in 1951, returning to Pisa when he was in his early sixties. As a disciplined militant, he never mentioned the existence of the report to anyone, and had no idea what had happened to it.

A decade later, Togliatti died in Yalta. On 25 August 1964, a vast funeral procession followed his bier in Rome. Within a few months, Athos Lisa's report was published in the PCI's weekly *Rinascita* on 12 December 1964, thirty years after it was written. Its author remained silent, dying soon afterwards in April 1965. Some time after his death, his widow found the manuscript of a memoir he had tucked away in the pages of an encyclopaedia, of which he had never spoken even to her. He must have completed it in the last months of his life, since it included the text of his report of 1933, of which he had possessed no copy since handing it over to Togliatti, and a note explaining why he omitted the opening sentences reproduced in *Rinascita*. Eventually, in 1973, the memoir was edited and published by the last survivor of Communist leadership born in the 1890s, the heterodox Umberto Terracini.[1] The text printed below is the fifth chapter

---

1 Athos Lisa, *Memorie. Dall'ergastolo di Santo Stefano alla Casa penale di Turi di Bari*, Milan 1973, with preface by Terracini.

of the book, containing both Lisa's report of Gramsci's lectures in prison and his description of what followed them in the conditions of each at Turi di Bari.

Kept secret when it was written, revealed only after the death of the leader who made sure it had remained so, the Athos Lisa report has not ceased to be explosive to this day. The reason why Togliatti concealed it in 1933 lay in what Gramsci called his 'punch in the eye' to the official line of the party: his call for a Constituent Assembly to rally all anti-fascist forces in Italy, as a transitional objective in the advance towards a socialist revolution for which the communist party did not yet command sufficient support to aim outright—this, at a time when the PCI leadership was propagating the delusions of the Third Period of the Comintern that revolution was around the corner and the only force against fascism was itself. After 1935, the Comintern switched to the strategy of a Popular Front, but since it did so without any allusion to its previous sectarian line, let alone self-criticism for it, Lisa's report had still to be suppressed, as damning evidence of past error and the fate that Togliatti had dealt Gramsci's rejection of it.

Within a decade of its release after Togliatti's death, however, the report became an embarrassment to the PCI, no longer as a deviation to the 'right' of the party's line, but as all too awkward evidence of how far Gramsci's politics were to the 'left' of it. Now proclaiming a peaceful, parliamentary road to a better future— ever more vaguely defined, references to socialism giving way to talk simply of a more 'advanced democracy', indistinguishable from traditional social-democratic parlance, the party had no less reason to want to occlude the report, since it made plain that Gramsci was fully committed to a violent overthrow of the capitalist state, setting out the kind of military organisation the party needed to create for this purpose, and treating hegemony in the classic Leninist acceptation of the term as the task of winning the peasantry and petty bourgeoisie as allies for the working class in its battle to sweep away the bourgeoisie. At the antipodes of the 'historic compromise' the PCI was seeking with the DC, the leading party of the Italian bourgeoisie, such conceptions were anathema to its recent transmogrification. Athos Lisa's report had now either to be ignored, as if it had never existed, or subjected to risible glosses, presenting it as—if read properly—a virtual anticipation of the party's current line, or finally as the work of a dim, doubtfully reliable cadre whose primitive understanding of Gramsci's ideas was also in part a function of Gramsci's need to dumb these down for the low intellectual level of his fellow prisoners.[2]

Ostensibly, in this cleansing of the past, the one idea in the Athos Lisa report to survive lustration is what originally made it too hot to handle in Paris. Gramsci had called for a Constituent Assembly in 1933, and in 1946 a Constituent Assembly there duly was, which wrote the Italian Constitution that today's descendant of the PCI, the Democratic Party of Matteo Renzi, has sought—but failed—to whittle down as too radical. Still, it might be asked, is not the larger fact that Gramsci's best political idea was vindicated by history, in the creation of as post-war Italian democracy of which his party was a key founder? The reality is more bitter. Gramsci, as he explained to others in prison, not only saw a Constituent Assembly as a way-station en route to a destination remote from anything envisaged by the party after

---

2    Illustrated, respectively, by Gianni Francioni, *L'officina gramsciana*, Naples 1984, *passim*, for which see above pp. 7–8; Angelo Rossi, *Gramsci da eretico a icona*, Naples 2010, pp. 95–115; Giuseppe Vacca, *Vita e pensieri di Antonio Gramsci*, Turin 2012, pp. 120–2 ff, for which see *The H-Word*, p. 81 n5.

the war. He stipulated that all who were heavily compromised by fascism should be excluded from its voting rolls. So far from anything like this occurring, no serious purge of any kind was made of fascist officials in the Italian state apparatus after 1945, when Togliatti was Minister of Justice, virtually every prefect, let alone subordinate, who had served Mussolini remaining in place. Among these officials was the very military judge, Enrico Macis, who had sent Gramsci to his martyrdom in prison. Promoted for his service to the regime in staging Gramsci's trial, along with that of many other Communists, Macis went on to military duties in Mussolini's conquest of Ethiopia and then the fascist seizure of Slovenia, annexed to Italy during the war. There he presided over deportations and repressions that earned him the highest praise of the generals in command of the Italian occupation, and a Slovene demand for his extradition as a war criminal after 1945. In post-war Italy, not a hair of his head was touched. He was even called upon for help in organising an anti-fascist exhibition in Milan, and lived out the rest of the days till 1973 in complete tranquillity.[3] At no point did the PCI lift a finger to expose him or bring him to justice. To read Lisa's description of what Gramsci endured at the hands of this figure is a reminder of what his party preferred to forget.

---

3  The merit of finally bringing this history to light belongs to Ruggero Giacomini, whose fine study *Il giudice e il prigionero*, Rome 2014, includes the fullest and best account, from a variety of witnesses, of Gramsci's years and views in prison. For his determination that fascists be struck off the rolls of a Constituent Assembly, see the testimony of Ercole Piacentini in Cesare Bermani, *Gramsci, gli intelletuali e la cultura proletaria*, Milan 2007.

## MEMOIR

When the number of political prisoners at Turi di Bari increased, our desire for some assessment of the situation in Italy and the party's line on it became more pressing, also because the new arrivals in prison brought us contradictory news of these. At first Gramsci didn't seem eager to express himself, not because he didn't have clear ideas on the subject but because of the objective difficulty of broaching such a complex subject in front of an audience as large as ours within a prison. To do so would have required many hours. Gramsci feared that this could draw the attention of the prison authorities, giving them an excuse for restrictive measures that would affect everyone. However, after having devised certain preventive measures to avoid alarming them, Gramsci finally decided to address the subject that was so close to his heart. For about a fortnight, during our time in the courtyard every morning, Gramsci spoke of Italy's political and economic situation, the relationship of forces and the international conjuncture, with such acuity and depth that he surprised even those who had heard him speak before his arrest.

When Gramsci began his report on the Italian and international situation he warned us that what he was about to tell us would be a kind of 'punch in the eye', since he would talk about the 'Constituent Assembly'.[4] At the time, his abrupt formulation and schematic treatment of this subject, in isolation from a series of questions that I felt could not be ignored without turning an essentially political problem into an academic argument, gave

---

4   Lisa's report follows, omitting a couple of initial sentences in which he noted that he was writing from memory two years after the event, so could not guarantee recalling every argument in Gramsci's complex thought, but had given as accurate and objective account of it as was in his power.

me the impression of a casual *boutade* thrown out to animate our daily discussions. Later I realised that Gramsci had planned his 'punch in the eye' quite deliberately, tackling many political problems both before and after he delivered it in the same spirit, with the same logic, to the same purpose. In fact, he told us that he had thought long and hard about the question of a Constituent Assembly, to which he attached the greatest political importance, since in his view it commanded the tactics the party should follow.

The opposition he expressed on this issue was preceded by two talks on 'intellectuals and the party' and 'the military problem and the party', whose basic ideas I will try to report since they struck me as closely connected with his conception of the Constituent Assembly, or at any rate allowed me to see the general train of his thought. In the first, Gramsci argued that intellectuals are absolutely necessary for the proletariat, both in historical periods when it is a class in-itself and in those when it is a class for-itself. Without intellectuals the proletariat could neither come to power, nor consolidate or develop its power after winning it. But who should be considered intellectuals, and among these, on whom should the party concentrate its work? The intellectuals of the working class, Gramsci said, are the elements that make up the vanguard of the proletariat: the party. In support of this idea Gramsci drew an analogy between the party and certain branches of bourgeois state organisation, taking its factories and armed services as examples. In both of these he classified those who exercise a function beyond mere execution of physical tasks as intellectuals or semi-intellectuals. In factories, he considered intellectuals all those—for example engineers or managers—responsible for putting into practice plans laid down in general form by the owner of the enterprise or its board. He classed as semi-intellectuals those in charge of the technical or administrative oversight of labour, for example superintendents, foremen, team leaders, clerks at various levels. In the army, he considered intellectuals all senior officers to whom the general staff assign the concretisation of tactical or strategic plans, and semi-intellectuals all those—NCOs and junior officers—responsible for seeing that these are executed correctly by the troops. In Gramsci's view, the organisation of the party, with its central committee above and its peripheral organisations below, followed the same model.

Defining intellectuals in this way by particular activities, Gramsci wanted to establish a sharp distinction between different social categories, in order to separate the kind of intellectual that could be of interest to the party from bourgeois intellectuals. Thus, following Gramsci's analysis, the directors and chief executives of companies, generals, leaders of philosophical schools etc. should be considered the purest representatives of the bourgeoisie.

Discussing 'the military problem and the party', Gramsci made it clear that the violent conquest of power necessitates the creation by the party of an organisation of a military type, pervasively implanted within every branch of the bourgeois state apparatus, and capable of wounding and inflicting heavy blows on it at the decisive moment of struggle. The problem of military organisation had to be understood, however, as part of the much wider work of the party, for this particular activity presupposed tight interdependence with the whole range of its practical actions and its ideological development. The purely technical aspect of military organisation was not to be considered in isolation. Decisive for its capability and efficacy was its political direction. Those in charge of it needed unusual qualities, which were in many ways a function of the ideological level of the party. An unconditional requirement of the proletarian revolution, Gramsci said, is a shift in the relations of armed force in favour of the working class. But by military relations of force should be understood not just possession of weapons or combat units, but the ability of the party to paralyse the nerve centres of the bourgeois state apparatus. For example: a general strike can shift the military relations of force in favour of the working class. Accurate intelligence of the strength of the enemy was also an indispensable condition of waging civil war. In an overview of the Italian military, he listed regular troops and specialised forces like the carabinieri, militia, state police and retired officers. He attributed great importance to this last category as a military and political force. Given Italy's geographical configuration, amongst the most important offensive weapons of the enemy he noted armoured trains. Running along the Adriatic or Ionian coast, these could immobilise and sow terror among the population, wherever the party had not created a military organisation capable in some measure of paralysing the operation of these powerful instruments of bourgeois action.

I mentioned that Gramsci presented his view of the issue of the 'Constituent Assembly' because he wanted to hear our ideas about it. Like other comrades who heard his exposition, I had the impression Gramsci attached a lot of importance to our response to his talk. He never tired of repeating that the party suffered from maximalism and that his work of political education among us aimed at creating a core of people capable of a healthier ideological contribution to it. Too often in the party, he said, there is a fear of anything that doesn't belong to the old maximalist phrasebook. People think the proletarian revolution is something that at a certain point arrives ready-made. Every

tactical move that doesn't conform to a dreamy subjectivism is
considered a distortion of the tactics and strategy of the revolution. So there is often talk about revolution without any precise
idea of what would be needed to bring it about, of the means
necessary to achieve it as an end, or how to adapt these means
to different historical situations. There was a general tendency to
elevate words over political action, or to confuse the two. That's
why Gramsci termed the issue of the Constituent Assembly a
'punch in the eye'.

His presentation of this theme focussed on two conceptions:
1) the tactics of winning allies for the proletariat; 2) the tactics
of winning power. He developed these roughly as follows. Italian
reaction, in depriving the proletariat of its party, class organisations, press, and any legal opportunity for meetings and strikes,
had stripped it of the most indispensable means of struggle for
a relatively rapid achievement of its hegemony as a class. Italy
was primarily an agricultural country marked by a great dispar-
ity between North and South in both its economic structures
and social layers within the labouring classes; the industrial
development in the South lagged behind that of the North even
as capital became more centralised; for historical reasons the
peasantry continued to be ideologically subordinate in some
degree to petty-bourgeois elements, who formed the best relay
for the agrarian bourgeoisie to keep down the peasantry. The
task for the Italian proletariat of winning over allied classes was
therefore extremely delicate and difficult. But without gaining
their support, the proletariat had no chance of building any
serious revolutionary movement. Given the particular historical conditions that had cramped the political development of
peasants and petty bourgeois in Italy, and the currently limited
possibilities for the party greatly to alter their political and

organisational backwardness, it was not hard to grasp that the party needed a line of action that, by unfolding in stages, became comprehensible and accessible to these social layers.

In present conditions of popular life and struggle, the peasant and especially the rural petty bourgeois were not capable of identifying with the Communist Party, or its slogans and ultimate aims. These social strata could come to a direct struggle for power only by stages: that is, if the party led them step by step to see the justice of its programme and the falsity of that of other political parties, in whose demagogy peasants and petty bourgeois still believed. Today it would be easy enough to convince a Southern peasant that the King was superfluous, but much harder that he could be replaced by a worker, just as he doesn't believe it would be possible for him to replace his master. A petty bourgeois or junior officer in the army, frustrated by precarious living conditions or lack of promotion, will more easily believe his lot would improve in a republican regime than a soviet system. The first step towards which these social strata needed to be guided was to express themselves on constitutional and institutional issues. Every worker, even the most backward peasant of Basilicata or Sardinia, now understood the uselessness of the monarchy.

On this terrain the party could join forces with other parties fighting against fascism in Italy, but should not tail them. The aim of the party was the violent conquest of power and establishment of the dictatorship of the proletariat, to be achieved by tactical adjustment to its historical situation and the balance of class forces in successive phases of the struggle. Assuming the party could navigate these, its political ability would then depend on a passage beyond its intermediate demands, as so many stages in unblocking the social strata it had to win over for a shift in the balance of forces. Yet even if the pressure of reaction in Italy slackened in the immediate future, action by the party would still face great difficulties. At best, it could count on no more than 6,000 active members. Divide that by the number of regions in Italy and the limits to its efficacy leapt to the eye. In conditions like these there could be no talk of conquering power without passing through a period of transition, however relatively limited its duration.

There were two scenarios for revolution in Italy, one more likely than the other. Gramsci held it that the most probable would involve a period of transition. The tactics of the party should envisage this without fear of appearing not very revolutionary. It should make the slogan of a Constituent Assembly its own, not as an end in itself but as a means, before any other anti-fascist party adopted it. The Assembly would offer an institutional framework for its representatives to pose the most urgent demands of the working class, to discredit every scheme for peaceful reform, and to show the Italian working class that the only viable solution for Italy lay in a proletarian revolution. Here Gramsci liked to recall the 'Association of Young Sardinia' of Turin in 1919, when well-judged and timely action by the Party had rallied the poor against the rich, enrolling them in the Sardinian socialist educational society within the chamber of trade unions. As a direct consequence, soldiers from the Sassari Brigade of the army had taken the side of Turin's working class. This, he said, was a bit like a small Constituent Assembly. He added that the first article in the Bolshevik programme for government had included the demand for a Constituent Assembly. To reach an agreement with the antifascist parties from a position of political independence and superior strength, the party must lay claim to the same idea. In this way our tactics would lead us, without worrying about labels, to achieve the aims the party had set itself.

Following a disagreement with me, Gramsci—who had so far not said at what point a Constituent Assembly could be realised—added he thought that as economic conditions in Italy worsened we would see sporadic but recurrent outbreaks of popular unrest, and this ferment would be the sign that a Constituent Assembly had become feasible in Italy. But the party should start calling for one right away. Since he assumed the objective conditions for a proletarian revolution had existed in Europe for over fifty years, comrade Gramsci's analysis set aside any assessment of the interdependence of the Italian economy with that of other capitalist states, the inherent consequences of the deepening world economic crisis, the radicalisation of the working class and disintegration in the social support of certain pseudo-proletarian (social-democratic) parties, or the political influence at large of the development of the Soviet economy. We must, he said, be more political, better able to act politically, less afraid of doing politics. Pausing incidentally to consider the slogan of 'workers' and peasants' government', he said that this was historically superseded and should be replaced by a 'republic of workers' and peasants' soviets in Italy'. This argument was not developed by Gramsci, but as far as I remember the implication was that the slogan 'workers' and peasants' government' had been appropriated by the pseudo-proletarian and democratic parties, suggesting a shift in their social base. I could not say whether Gramsci meant that this shift had pushed these parties to the left, or simply to a more demagogic phraseology.

After Gramsci's presentation, we were invited to express our own opinions on the call for a Constituent Assembly. Each, within the limits of their ability, said what they thought and on the whole nearly everyone agreed with Gramsci's positions. Those in favour were comrades Tulli, Lai, Piacentini, Ceresa, Spadoni, Lo Sardo and a few others whose names I don't exactly recall. Those against were Scucchia from Rome and myself. Nevertheless, at Gramsci's express wish, all those present at the discussion were invited to reconsider the question and come back to say what they thought a fortnight later. This never happened because Gramsci, under the influence of false information, thought that discussions among comrades put in separate sections of the prison were becoming factional.

At a brief meeting Gramsci announced that he would suspend ongoing conversations among comrades for six months because political education was lacking. So the question of the 'Constituent Assembly' was born and died in Turi di Bari, while it remained alive in the mind of comrade Gramsci—so much so that in October 1932 he spoke of it to me with the same deep conviction and enthusiasm he had shown in 1930.

The day after Gramsci's presentation I asked him to set out his view of fascism—what he thought were the historical conditions that had produced it, what interests it represented and where its social composition lay. I felt that our perspectives on the Italian situation could not be objective without a clear understanding of all this. Gramsci agreed to my proposal and the next day outlined a retrospective history of fascism that I will try to summarise as succinctly as I can, to avoid distorting Gramsci's ideas amid details.

Here is what he argued:

Fascism as we see it in Italy is a peculiar form of bourgeois reaction which emerged out of specific historical conditions of the bourgeoisie in general and our country in particular. Italian fascism could not be accurately understood without situating it in the history of the Italian people, and the economic and political structures of Italy. If we want a more grounded explanation of the particular features of the form of reaction called fascism in Italy, we have to go back, at least, to the historical matrices of successive stages in the unification of the Italian state, to the nefarious influence of the church, to the actions of democracy and social democracy. The lack of any political unity of the Italian bourgeoisie, rooted in the economic structure of our country, and conspicuous during the period of struggles for Italian independence, accounts in good part for the origin and development of fascism, which acquired the function of uniting all bourgeois forces, once the historical conditions were ripe for doing so.

Conversely, the absence of any true bourgeois–democratic revolution in Italy, which left unsolved a whole series of problems whose resolution would have given greater cohesion to the Italian bourgeoisie, sharpened the class struggle and accelerated the development of the proletariat. If by participating in the First World War the Italian bourgeoisie seemed to achieve a unity it had never before known, the post-war period reopened all the contradictions that the war had in part attenuated, reproducing in exacerbated form all the old problems of Italian society. This was a historical moment defined by what could be called a parallelism between the forces ranged against each other. On one side the bourgeois forces fought without any political unity to impose the costs of the war on the working class, while on the other the working class led by the Socialist Party fought for the conquest of power without itself having achieved any class unity. But while the Italian proletariat, misled by the Socialist Party, diluted its revolutionary potential in tactics that did not lead to the conquest of power, the bourgeoisie succeeded in regrouping its forces to combat the working class.

The first phase of the fascist movement, which began with violent squads paid by landowners in some agricultural areas and particularly the Po Valley, was an expression of the bourgeois struggle against workers in general and in particular the struggle of the rural bourgeoisie against the association of agricultural labourers. The tactics of the Italian bourgeoisie followed two trajectories: one aimed against the trade unions and the other against the Federterra. The arrow of its attack, however, started in the countryside before turning on the cities, reversing the traditional throttling of Italian rural society by the towns. At first, the elements active in the fascist organisations were recruited from the dregs of society. In a second phase, after Giolitti's government lent its support, they came from the rural and urban petty bourgeoisie, which believed that its turn had come to determine the future of Italy. This moment coincided with a broadening of the social bases of fascism, and a subsidence of the revolutionary impetus that had found expression in the movement of factory occupations. All further developments in the political struggle in Italy reflected, through the prism of tumultuous and contradictory actions of the Fascist Party, phases in the conflict between the proletariat and the action–reaction of the social classes deployed by the bourgeoisie against it. This process moved more or less in parallel with a centralisation of capital in Italy resulting in the dominance of finance capitalism, to the interests of which the politics of fascism became subordinate.

Thus at a certain moment fascism became the form of organisation called upon to defend the interests of this sector of the Italian bourgeoisie, while at the same time managing, to a certain degree and by various means, to mitigate differences among the interests of the class as a whole. This performance was facilitated by the anti-democratic character of so many Italian institutions, including a legal system that inhibited any possibility of checking the overweening power of the strongest economic groups, a parliament subject to the discretionary powers of the king, a judiciary that was non-elective, and so on.

Along with this centralisation of the forces of the bourgeoisie had come, moving at a much slower pace, a radicalisation of the working class—a process of which the Communist Party and its ideology was in part an expression. Although fascism had failed completely in its aim of resolving the economic crisis, it did allow the Italian bourgeoisie to overcome the deep political crisis of the post-war years without too much turbulence, achieving a relative stabilisation of its position. Of course this was at the expense of the working class. Though so far contained, the Italian economic crisis would certainly deepen, with consequences already visible in worker and peasant unrest, and rising economic and political discontent. The objective conditions for a conquest of power by the proletariat were already all there. But these were not enough. Wide layers of the masses—especially peasant—lacked the political maturity of workers. The influence of pseudo-proletarian socialist parties and cliques had not yet been destroyed. The party faced the urgent problem of achieving the hegemony of the proletariat, without which the conquest of power would be impossible. It should be prepared for the bourgeoisie to take extreme measures in its own defence, which in Italy might go as far as conceding land to the peasantry. The greatest problem remained the correlation of class forces. Taking account of its specificities in our country, the party's action should aim at rapidly shifting the balance of power in favour of the working class.

In summarising Gramsci's ideas, I have relied on the accuracy of my memory, setting aside any sectarian element and trying not to invalidate them with my own views. I cannot guarantee I have reported exactly everything Gramsci told us two and a half years ago. Whoever reads and wants to discuss the findings in this report should bear that in mind.[5]

I never heard Gramsci talk about the policies of the party. Whenever one asked him about these, he answered without hesitation: 'I think the party's line is correct.' Yet his analysis of the Italian situation implied it was not correct. That made us uneasy, leaving us with a deep disillusion rather than a stimulus to reflect and discuss. The obvious contrast between the political line pursued by the party and the course Gramsci proposed as the only effective way to fight fascism was unacceptable to some of us, despite our respect and affection for Gramsci.

Lo Sardo, who had contracted nephritis in jail, was visibly declining.[6] Aware of his condition, he requested that he be allowed to die among his relatives. The Ministry of the Interior, through the prison authorities, let him know he could do so if he made an act of submission to the regime. The disdain with which this comrade, who was then about seventy-five, treated that reply surprised those of us who loved him and would have forgiven him such an act, if it allowed him to live a couple more years. Lo Sardo chose to stay in prison and watch himself slowly die rather than ask for clemency. Lai, who was closest to him, took care of him like a loving son, but this could not be enough for someone as ill as Lo Sardo. At times during our hours in the courtyard, I would call him to play chequers with me, on a board we would draw on the stone bench with a piece of brick, and purposely let him win. This made Lo Sardo very happy because

---

5   Here ends the report by Lisa published in *Rinascita*.
6   Francesco Lo Sardo (1871–1931): Socialist militant from Sicily, who became the first communist deputy for the island in 1924.

he took it to mean that his mental faculties were not diminished. But that was not so. Eventually he was taken to hospital, where this valiant fighter, of a stainless loyalty to the working class, died. Tulli held a memorial for him in the courtyard of the prison where Gramsci and the rest of us stood in homage. Another fighter, the oldest among us, had left us forever. His legacy was the battles he had fought with an ardour typical of the noble land of Sicily, and the example he set of how to uphold an idea for which he sacrificed his life.

Soon after our discussions of the Italian political situation, Bruno Tosin arrived in Turi di Bari. When a new comrade entered our prison, he was always greeted as a messenger from the outside world who for a few days brightened the life of those sentenced before him. We wanted to know so many things and ask so many questions, but above all we wanted news of what was happening in Italy, of the work of the party, and of the prospects for the fall of fascism. Tosin had been a party functionary, who before his arrest had worked together with Camilla Ravera in Turin. He was a well-trained comrade who had followed a course in the Leninist school and served as a party cadre for years. He could therefore give us important political and economic information, tell us to what extent the party's policy was being applied by workers, what forces we had at our disposal in the country, how the party saw the future of fascism.

The information Tosin gave us was not that different from what we already knew, but what astounded us was his claim that the party expected the revolution by the end of the year. We did not hide our disbelief in this flattering prediction, and asked him to tell Gramsci what he had said to us. The following day Gramsci, whom we had already alerted, met Tosin. He asked Tosin when and where he had been arrested, how long his sentence was, where he had been active before his arrest. As Tosin answered these first questions, Gramsci's expression became more attentive, almost stern. Then he suddenly asked, 'How many active comrades were there in Turin and the province when you were working there?' Tosin thought a moment, then replied, 'Perhaps a hundred.' At this Gramsci's face contracted in an expression typical of him at a moment of severity. Without further ado, he asked Tosin, taking his arm in a friendly gesture, 'So you wanted to make the revolution with that number of communists?' Tosin looked as if struck by an electric shock and couldn't answer. Gramsci was not the sort of comrade who, after expressing a stern opinion (which in this case did not just concern Tosin), would leave a comrade humiliated or offended. He continued to talk to Tosin about different topics as if nothing had occurred. But the expression on his face suggested that he had not recovered his usual calm.

Gramsci's analysis of the Italian and international situation had split the comrades in Turi into two opposing camps and triggered an intense, passionate discussion in our cells and in the exercise yard. It was not unusual or abnormal for comrades to have political discussions, nor did this surprise the prison guards. But Gramsci took another view, fearing these discussions would create actual fractions among us. Piacentini and Ceresa must have encouraged this completely unfounded fear by distorting our discussions, whose purpose was essentially to clarify problems Gramsci had raised and about which none of us had settled opinions. Thus just when we were preparing to put some of our conclusions to Gramsci, he summoned us and said he was suspending all further discussion for six months to prevent the emergence of fractions. This announcement disappointed all those who had heard Gramsci speak, because it denied us the chance to continue a discussion that would have helped us clarify our views on some aspects of the line Gramsci thought the party ought to pursue, and certainly did not lessen resentments brewing, especially among the youngest prisoners, for reasons that were not always political. Was this the real reason why Gramsci punished our group by depriving it of the chance to discuss an issue about which he had said he wanted to know what we thought?

In my view, the most probable explanation for his decision lay in the state of his health, and the rule he had given himself of following prison regulations to the letter, to avoid being transferred to another section, or still worse sent to another prison. This conjecture may seem illogical, but it is entirely possible given Gramsci's state of health at the time. His insomnia had become more intense, even incurable, despite strong doses of sedatives. The midnight inspection of our cells woke him up and for the rest of the night he couldn't fall asleep again. The prison authorities took some measures to make the inspections less noisy, but these were of little help. The truth is that Gramsci's health worsened day by day. The first signs of this deterioration came when he repeatedly started to cough up blood, against which the remedies available in prison could do very little. Gramsci would have needed to be transferred to a sanatorium in a supportive environment to have a chance of recovering. Turi was not such a place, even though he was able to receive medicines brought to him by his sister-in-law Tatiana.

Moreover, sitting at a table for as many hours as he did during the day worsened his physical condition. At times we advised him to rest during the day, but he wouldn't listen to us. I consider myself, he said, at the editorial desk of *L'Ordine Nuovo* and I need to write an article every day. The range of topics he treated reflects that reply, in my view. Gramsci certainly wished to provide or suggest original solutions for Italian problems, to help the Italian movement move forward politically along the lines that he had often indicated. His discussion of problems of Fordism was in effect a reply to positions adopted by the honourable comrade Riboldi in Turi di Bari, who after reading a few books by Ford decided that Fordism was tantamount to social-ism.[7] Since Riboldi was writing a book on the subject there is no doubt that he prompted Gramsci to compose what he probably would have said about it in *L'Ordine Nuovo*. We could guess what Gramsci was writing, and why he felt such a strong desire to write, but he offered no further explanation. He told no-one about what he was actually writing. He just said he was writing about Benedetto Croce, or the function of intellectuals, or the Vatican, but without entering into the problems he wanted to address in doing so. Did he consider his comrades ill-equipped to discuss them, or was he silent because he feared his work might be compromised by some indiscretion that could reach the ears of the prison authorities? I think the second hypothesis is closer to the truth.

Objectively speaking, Gramsci did not trust any comrade. Not that he thought anyone capable of reporting to the authorities the actual content of what he was writing, which he anyway sought to camouflage with elusive turns of phrase, and of which few comrades even knew in the first place. It was because the atmos-phere in prison created systematic feelings of distrust towards everything, especially in Gramsci's case when his general physi-cal condition and state of health were so precarious. Gramsci

---

7   Ezio Riboldi: former Socialist deputy in the Italian Parliament, who joined the Communist Party and was imprisoned in the twenties; amnestied and expelled from the PCI in 1933.

felt an absolute need to remain in Turi di Bari and didn't want to risk being transferred to another prison. He was the head of the Communist Party and knew how close was the surveillance which he was under and how many risks he ran every day. Looked at this way, we can understand and justify his diffidence towards men and things.

I was struck down by a fever the two doctors in the prison diagnosed as typhoid. Since political prisoners could not use the prison infirmary, the cell I shared with Riboldi and Pertini had to do, though it lacked the most elementary means of looking after a patient whose temperature was running at 40–1 degrees. With the approval of the prison authorities, Pertini and Lai, to whom I owe so much for their affection, took it in turns to look after me day and night, providing care which I certainly would not have enjoyed in the prison infirmary.[8] But I lay ill for several months and my condition worsened every day. Pertini had to argue with doctor Cisternino, who was the Fascist Party secretary in Turi di Bari, and regularly expressed surprise that I never became delirious despite sky-high temperatures. This doctor, who stammered, had limited medical knowledge, and was a mean-spirited and sectarian fascist to boot. One morning he repeated his habitual refrain that I should have fallen into delirium. 'His mind continues to be clear,' he said. To which Pertini replied, 'Clearer than yours.' An altercation ensued and Pertini all but ended up in solitary confinement once again. The comrades in Turi, worried about my state of health, asked the directorate of the prison to transfer me to a hospital, but when

8    Sandro Pertini (1896–1990): Socialist who went on to play a leading role in the resistance, becoming a deputy and senator for the PSI after the war, and eventually president of the republic (1978–1985). Giovanni Lai: Sardinian communist, active in Cagliari and member of the Central Committee after the war.

the authorisation came from the Ministry I was no longer in a fit state to be transported. I could tell that my condition was critical because I kept receiving visits from the local parish priest, though I had neither called nor encouraged him, and from the chief warder who every night came to see if I was still alive. The prison authorities had already informed my family of my condition, so all formalities were completed for my passage to the afterlife.

My family would not have been able to come from Livorno to Turi di Bari had Pertini not secured the money for them to make the trip. A friar, who was a friend of Pertini's mother and often came to Turi to see him and bring him news of her, was entrusted with this mission and my family received the means to come and see me. My sisters arrived in Turi accompanied by a professor from the University of Bari recommended by friends who lived there. It was this visit by my sisters that cancelled my trip to the other world. In the presence of the two prison doctors, the chief warder and my sisters, I received a quick diagnosis that left everybody surprised, especially the two doctors in charge of me. 'What illness are you treating him for?' asked the professor. 'Typhoid fever,' mumbled the doctors. The professor made a gesture of dismissal and said that the graph of my temperature should have told them I had Malta fever. Without further discussion he suggested how I should be cured. No more ice (I consumed 18kg per day) nor enemas nor diet. They must feed me immediately, starting with a fourth of an egg yolk a day and progressively giving me more food. If there was a garden, I should be taken out to breathe fresh air. The dear professor, whose name I have forgotten, had plainly never been to prison or he would have understood that certain privileges are not granted to inmates.

Gramsci followed the progress of my illness with the same anxiety and affection shown me by other comrades. One day he peered at the small window in my cell door and stretched his arm inside, passing me a small bouquet of flowers that he had grown and picked in a little corner of the courtyard where we exercised. 'How are you?' he asked, and after wishing me a speedy recovery went back to his cell. This was an unusual gesture for a man like Gramsci, who was not sentimental. But prison, rather than stifling or drying up affections, encourages their demonstration, especially towards comrades. It brings together those who have been deprived of liberty to defend the same idea, the same conception of the world. It is not true at all that a need to defend one's own life produces forms of selfishness that extinguish solidarity, which a common life in prison actually reinforces. My illness lingered a long time for all the cures I underwent. My fever dropped, but did not disappear, so that in the end I was transferred to another prison where I could benefit from a radical change of climate.

*Translated by Eleanor Chiari*

# INDEX